ONE GOD. ONE PLAN.
ONE FAMILY…

LIVING THE MESSAGE

ONE GOD. ONE PLAN.
ONE FAMILY…

LIVING THE
MESSAGE

MAURICE JONES

Matador
9 De Montfort Mews
Leicester LE1 7FW, UK
Tel: (+44) 116 255 9311 / 9312
Email: books@troubador.co.uk
Web: www.troubador.co.uk/matador

ISBN 978-1905886-296

Typeset in 11pt Bembo by Troubador Publishing Ltd, Leicester, UK
Printed by The Cromwell Press Ltd, Trowbridge, Wilts, UK

Matador is an imprint of Troubador Publishing Ltd

For my wife Angie, who is more precious to me than she will ever know, and for Ben, Emily and Simeon, who have enriched my life beyond measure.

INTRODUCTION

When God has something special to say, sometimes He uses miracles to communicate the message. Sometimes world events. Sometimes ordinary people. Sometimes ordinary families.

Following God, as a Christian, is never an easy option, but it becomes profound when you discover that He has used your successes, your failures, your marriage, your family as a means of conveying His message to others.

God did not give us the choice of opting out, we would have said no. So we have lived out our life as a family, not knowing its significance. Until now.

When God speaks, it always has a context. He talks to different generations in ways that are familiar to them. In language that is relevant to their time, their circumstances, their needs and aspirations. So what is God's message to His church and society, in the 21st century?

To understand the message it is helpful to understand a little about the messengers. To discover how God has influenced our thinking, our beliefs, our lifestyle. To discern how His message has been woven into our lives and fashioned by events and those with whom we have had close contact. This book seeks to achieve that.

Why did God choose us? Only He knows. But something in our lives caught His attention.

God's message has been birthed in the ordinary, but if listened to and acted upon, its impact will change the world.

People say 'God is dead.' Don't believe them.

Special thanks to all those who know us so well, but whose names we have been unable to include in the text. Your contribution to our lives has not been forgotten.

CHAPTER ONE

The Journey Begins....

Emily Elizabeth Patience Jones died on Thursday 26th September 1985. She was four years, six months old.

The driver of the articulated lorry that smashed into our car had never deliberately meant to cause us harm.

I have, on occasions, driven over the speed limit myself, and on that day, for a variety of reasons, the lorry driver had done the same. His sudden need to brake hard had caused the trailer to swerve across the road directly into our path.

Neither I, nor Angie, my wife have any recollection of the accident, but drivers following us told the police that our Fiat 127 hatchback had simply 'exploded' as we collided, without warning, with the rear of the lorry.

We had just passed the cottage hospital in Sudbury, Suffolk where our son, Ben and daughter, Emily had both been born, when our journey was cut tragically short.

The front of the car on the driver's side was completely crushed and onlookers, fearing the car may ignite, had frantically broken the car windows and pulled us clear of the wreckage. Angie, Ben and I were rushed by ambulance to the intensive care unit in the West Suffolk Hospital, Bury St Edmunds, whilst Emily, who had sustained multiple abdominal and head injuries, was en route for Addenbrookes Hospital,

Cambridge. During the journey, however, Emily's condition deteriorated and, having never regained consciousness, she died in the ambulance.

At the West Suffolk Hospital, Ben underwent emergency surgery on his duodenum and Angie received treatment for severe bruising to many parts of her body. I was taken straight to the operating theatre and treated for a fractured skull and a broken right leg.

It was three or four days later that I regained consciousness and woke to find myself on the intensive care ward. It was the first time I had been in hospital since I had had my tonsils removed as a child. That experience had not been reassuring. When offered Welsh Rabbit for tea I had concluded rabbit would not be to my liking and instead had chosen boiled fish. I did not really like fish either and secreted most of it away in a bag of grapes. The ruse worked well until the fish began to smell. I feared the wrath of the nursing staff and their retribution for wasting hospital food. The day I was discharged home a weight was lifted from my shoulders. But this time, when discharged from hospital care, there would be no lifting of the burden. No happy homecoming.

As I became aware of my surroundings I asked to know the details of what had befallen us. Words, at times like this, have little meaning and it was not until we visited the hospital mortuary and saw Emily's frozen body that reality became real.

It was odd, however, for considering the extent of her injuries, Emily was strangely unmarked. In fact, outwardly, perfect in every respect, but dead. Like a statue. So near yet so far away. Our tears and prayers could not revive her. The body was empty. Emily had already left this world and so had our hearts. On that one day, in that fraction of time, the future for Angie, Ben and I had changed for ever. From now on, nothing would ever be the same. Our priorities had been rearranged in an instant. Life, that gift we often take for granted and assume that for a child will go on way beyond the time-span of its parents, had suddenly become very, very precious.

Emily was beautiful (like her mother). She was smart (like her mother). She had a cheeky grin (like her mother). She had lovely brown eyes (like her father). She was in love (with her brother).

We had called her Patience because she was overdue when she was born.

She had a wonderful sense of fun and often had times of helpless giggling. When Emily laughed, so did everyone else. She had 'mischief' written in her eyes. You could see what she was thinking and you knew trouble was on the way. From an early age she had established some very close friendships. At playgroup, she and Katie had become inseparable. Emily with long brown hair and Katie with short, blonde, curly hair. They had appeared on stage together in a nativity play as two angels. To Angie and I that summed up Emily. She was our little angel.

Whenever I put her to bed, Emily would place both her arms around my neck and pull my head down so that she could kiss me on the cheek.

But Emily's relationship with Ben was special. From the beginning they had thoroughly enjoyed each others' company. They would talk together and play together. In the summer months they would gather straw bales together in the field next to our home and make 'dens'. Sometimes they would both sit in the wheelbarrow and I would race them around the garden. When they bathed together, they would splash and sing and blow soap bubbles.

Ben recalls, 'I have a few vivid memories of my sister and I know that we got on really well. I remember entering some fancy dress competitions with Em. One particular competition was when I dressed up as a cowboy and Em dressed up as a red indian – we didn't win, but it was fun. I also remember teaming up with Em on holiday to play 'it' with my Dad. We were in a barn on the top of a stack of straw bales. We would look over the edge to see where my Dad was below. I pushed a bale from off of the top to try and hit my Dad.

I remember when Em cut her hand on a cat food tin while she was trying to open it. I know she had to go and have stitches, but at the time I didn't realise how serious it was.

I remember really looking forward to Em joining my primary school. Being older I had had to go to school and leave my sister behind at home, but when I found out that she was going to be joining too I was over the moon. Em came to school a few times after the summer holidays and really enjoyed it. She never came to school again.

I remember being in the hospital and being asked by my parents if I wanted to see Em. I did. I went into the room and she was lying on the hospital bed. It was gloomy with some sunshine coming through the window on to her. She was wearing her blue dress with small white and red and orange flowers on it. She didn't look injured in any way she just looked like she was asleep. She looked peaceful and content.'

A week before our accident, Emily had been a bridesmaid at her Aunt Julie's wedding. Angie and I were not sure whether it was the excitement, but on the day, Emily had not seemed herself. After the ceremony, she had become sleepy and breathless and, as our concern grew we had decided to leave the reception early and request an emergency appointment with a local doctor. On examination he concluded she was having a severe asthma attack, and immediately called for an ambulance. In the back of the ambulance Emily was given oxygen to try and revive her. Angie recalls on arrival at Colchester General Hospital, 'I watched my little daughter being carried by a strong ambulance driver along a hospital corridor with her arms wrapped around his neck. I felt helpless.'

With the help of a nebulizer Emily recovered, and by the next morning was beginning to smile again. We had both felt such a sense of relief and joy as we realised how close we had come to losing her.

The next day was a Sunday and Angie and Emily had ventured out of the children's ward and found the empty hospital chapel. They had decided to have their own 'church service'. Having shared a prayer, Angie had said to Emily, 'What shall we sing to God?'

'Run Rabbit, Run Rabbit' had been her instant reply. So together they sang the song, knowing that it was probably not quite the usual type of tune He was offered, but hoping that God would enjoy it nevertheless.

4   MAURICE JONES

A few days later Emily was discharged from hospital, and we began to pack for a holiday we were destined never to enjoy.

The sudden death of a child is an unnerving experience for a parent. It confronts you with questions most people rarely ask. What is the meaning of life? What happens when we die? Why is life so unfair? It also deprives you not only of the present, the immediate pleasure of a touch, a kiss, a smile, but also the future. The romance of a first date, the stress of exam results, the excitement of a new job, the joy of grandchildren.

When an older person dies, although there is natural sadness, there can also be a sense of fulfilment. That they have lived a 'full life' and completed all that they wanted to achieve. Hopefully with few regrets. Indeed, there are those who are so content with life that they welcome death. They embrace it.

We did not welcome Emily's death. It came like a thief in the night. An unwelcome intruder who had broken in and stolen the plans of our life. Those dreams and aspirations that are locked away in every parent's mind. Emily's death was not part of the script. Our accident had released us from someone we did not want to let go. She was ours. Not that we owned her as such. She was not our possession. But neither was she a child that had been brought into existence for our convenience, a fashion statement, a 'must have' item on the shopping list of life. She was a gift to us and we loved her very much.

We would have been more than happy to have lived out our lives as an ordinary family, doing ordinary things, achieving what we could in our own innocent way. But Emily's death changed all that. Our beliefs on which we based so much of our lives were now under scrutiny. Either they were completely real and trustworthy or fraudulent and false.

The next three weeks in hospital saw the three of us trying to come to terms with our situation and slowly recovering from our injuries. The questions came thick and fast, with, "Why us?" taking priority. We were just an average family, no different from millions of families the world over.

Why us? When Angie and I both professed a Christian faith and we had tried hard for years to live in a way of which God, we felt, would approve. Why us and not somebody else? Why had the accident happened to us and not someone who was a 'bad' parent, or who had lots of children?

Why us? That was a good question and we needed a straight answer. We did not believe in fate or chance but divine planning and intervention. But where was God on that Thursday morning, and why did He not protect us?

Why?

CHAPTER TWO

Neither of our backgrounds gave any clues.

Angie was North Essex born and bred, the eldest of three sisters and one brother. She had spent much of her early childhood living on a farm and had grown to love open spaces and the delights of nature.

Over the years she had developed an intuitive artistic ability and also had a keen sense of fun that caused many friends and relatives to be on the receiving end of numerous, inventive practical jokes.

In September 1965 Angie had commenced her secondary education at Colchester High School for Girls, from where she moved in 1972 to a teacher training college in Bognor Regis, West Sussex. It was whilst Angie was training to be a teacher that her path crossed with mine.

I was born in 1952 in Hounslow, Middlesex a short distance from Heathrow Airport. I had lived with my mother and father, a self-employed painter, later a postman, and a younger brother, in a pre-war semi-detached house. When I was seven, my mother had sent me along to Sunday school in a nearby Anglican church and, two years later, I had become a regular member of a local Boys' Brigade Company, where I had learnt the fine arts of camping and bugle playing.

I was 16 years old when my parents moved house to Bognor Regis, where I completed my secondary education in the local comprehensive school.

At the age of twelve, at a Boys' Brigade camp on the Isle of Wight, I had innocently asked Jesus to 'come into my life' and had tried, in practical living to work out what that meant. I regularly read my Bible, prayed and attended a local evangelical church. I had never been radical, but felt that the Christian way of life did have a lot to commend it.

Following our move to Bognor, I decided to be baptised by immersion in water, although at the time I was unsure of its relevance to my faith, and part of my motive was to be like my Christian friends.

Not long after my baptism, I had attended a Christian meeting in a flat in Littlehampton. The leader invited anyone who wanted to 'receive the Spirit' to join him in the next room where he would 'lay hands' on them. I knew that in the Bible the Holy Spirit was a part of the Godhead (i.e. God the Father, God the Son and God the Holy Spirit) and that as the early Christian church began to grow, the church leaders would pray that converts would actually experience God's Holy Spirit living in them.

I knew in my heart it was the right thing to do, but I was nervous of the consequences. The battle raged in my mind for at least forty minutes until logic won the day. I remained seated where I was. I was nervous and I had received scant teaching on the need for the power of the Holy Spirit in the lives of Christians to help them live as God desires. In fact, it was only years later I learnt that 'becoming a Christian' had nothing to do with living in a 'Christian' country, or trying to live a 'Christian' life, or even attending a church. It was not a one-off decision, but a process, involving repentance, belief in the Lord Jesus through faith, baptism as a believer by immersion in water and receiving the Holy Spirit.

During my late teens I critically examined my faith and found that it lacked vibrancy and relevance to a modern world. Life was full of far more interesting things to do than sitting in a church on a Sunday morning. My Christian life went into decline.

Although during my last year at school I had expressed a vague notion of wanting to 'work with people' as a career, this only began to take shape when, in 1972, I commenced a two year diploma course in

Bromley, Kent with a view to entering social work.

One Saturday, shortly after the commencement of my course, I was invited by a friend to attend a Christian concert in London. At the end of the concert he introduced me to a young man called Mick Frisby. I had never met a Christian like Mick. He was the right person at the right time and for the next two years he helped me rediscover how dynamic Christianity can be. He gave me numerous opportunities to inflict my self-penned songs, all written in the same three guitar chords, on gracious audiences and the chance to preach at a special Sunday evening church anniversary service. The church was full, but my preaching was so uninspiring even I got bored!

Mick also helped me to learn to trust God. I had had a number of girlfriends during my teenage years and had twice wanted to get engaged to different girls. In their wisdom they had rejected me. I had eventually said to God, 'Okay, I am making a mess of my life and others. I am happy for you to do what you think is best for me'.

Some months later while I was on a weekend home visit, I attended our local church. The service had already started. At this stage in my life, my time-keeping was so bad my friends had nicknamed me, 'The late Maurice Jones'. I therefore squeezed, as unobtrusively as possible, into one of the back rows and found myself sharing a hymn book with a young lady I had not met before.

That chance meeting had little impact on me, but for Angie the rest of the service was a 'blur.' My shoulder length hair, smile and twinkling brown eyes convinced her that I was Mr Right. All she can remember is collecting her bike at the end of the service and cycling back to her lodgings saying, 'He'll do, God. He'll do!'

Angie's 'conversion' experience had been similar to mine, in that, during her teens whilst a member of a church youth group, she had asked God to become a part of her daily living. In the years that followed, she had been baptised by immersion and experienced the powerful moving of the Holy Spirit in herself and others. This, in turn, had fostered a desire in her to know Jesus more intimately. That intimate love relationship with Jesus had given her a spiritual maturity beyond her years. When she saw me, she knew.

Love eventually opened my eyes and six weeks later we became engaged.

It was to be another year before we got married as Angie still had to complete her teacher training. But in the meantime, I moved in to live with Angie's family and started a job with a land drainage company.

Love does strange things to you. You try to act rationally, but sometimes it just doesn't work.

On 31st October 1974 Angie wrote in her diary, 'Party began at 8-0... Bar BQ went very well – food great. A bit noisy – but good evening – then Mogsy came...just to support me...drove 260 miles...there and back... beautiful... as I write this he's driving home again... what a lovely thing love is!!'

And on 31st December she wrote, 'It's been an important year...met Mogs...consequent spiritual upset...and emotional traumas...still – once we have learned to adjust to each other then it'll all have been worth it. I'd have never thought that by now I'd be engaged and have short hair!'

Since her childhood, Angie had always wished to return to living in a house with oak beams and doors with latches and during that year, we purchased a two bedroom terraced cottage in a village near Colchester, Essex. Although being on a main road 'Pegtile Cottage' was our first home and having to duck through doorways, climb a near vertical staircase to access the bedroom and share a larder with mice, didn't bother us at all.

We were not yet sure, however, how we were going to pay the mortgage as Angie had not yet found a job.

A few days before the completion of her course in June 1975, Angie, while sitting in the student's union lounge, happened to pick up a three week old newspaper. In it was advertised a job teaching art, in a comprehensive school five miles away from our newly acquired home. The fact that she had trained as a Middle School teacher did not prove to be a barrier. She was offered and accepted the appointment.

One week after her 21st birthday, on July 19th Angie and I married in the village where she had spent most of her childhood. We made our vows and promised to keep them to the best of our ability. Like most people, though, we hoped our married life would err on the side of 'better', 'for richer' and 'in health'.

Angie's agricultural roots determined that, rather than travelling from the church to the reception in a limousine, we made the journey on the back of a trailer, pulled by a tractor. As we rode through the village sitting on bales of straw, so people came out of their houses to wave. It was the nearest I have ever come to understanding what it must be like to be royalty.

With no money for a honeymoon, after the reception we returned to our cottage and began to learn to live as one. We had our Christian principles to use as a foundation for our marriage, but wisdom can come from the most unexpected places.

In 1972 a singer/song writer named Stevie Wonder released an album, called 'Talking Book' (Tamla Motown). One of the songs entitled 'You and I' became a special favourite of ours. One line in particular has remained with me over the years — 'I only pray that I have shown you a brighter day.'

I have tried, often unsuccessfully, to put into practice those words in my daily relationship with Angie. As a motto for a marriage, it would be hard to find better.

During the first few weeks we slowly adjusted to each others' individual habits. Fortunately we quickly learnt that we needed to blend our backgrounds together and accept that our own personal way of doing things could be improved upon. And what did it matter anyway, if one of us was cautious and the other adventurous or one had a passion for beetroot and rhubarb and the other cottage cheese, as long as a balance was struck and agreement was reached on important issues.

We did not find it difficult to 'cleave' to each other, but it was in helping our parents to understand 'leaving' means allowing children to have the space to develop as a couple, that took time to resolve.

Angie commenced her teaching career in September. On the first day, during the initial assembly, she was allocated class 5J. These 15/16 year olds were considerably taller than she was and in order to gain some authority, she quickly got them seated and then sat on the highest desk she could find. The ploy worked. The class were under her control.

But it was only a partial success. Later that day an older teaching colleague ordered her out of the staff room, mistaking her for a sixth former!

Angie's Head of Department, though, was inspirational and taught her that by using humour, pupil engagement, positive reinforcement and a passion for the subject, even disenchanted children could be encouraged to participate in the education process.

During the next year, Angie and I began running a youth group in a local church hall. We enjoyed building relationships with the young people and trying to find creative ways of sharing our faith and keeping them entertained!

As far as we know, none of them became Christians. Indeed, some of them went on to pursue vandalism and petty crime as a means of filling their time, but hopefully some seeds for the future were sown.

Once a week, Angie and I would visit our local pub. As there were rarely many people in the restaurant, we felt the publican might appreciate our custom. Our spending money and the menu were both limited, but for £1 per order we could buy either a cheese omelette and chips or a mushroom omelette and chips. Being newly married, and wanting to share everything; each week we ordered one cheese and one mushroom omelette, cut them in half and slipped the halves from one plate to the other.

In April 1976, I was made redundant from the land drainage company and spent three months unemployed. In August, I commenced work as a trainee Local Authority Social Worker. I had a varied caseload, including people of all ages. Some had physical disabilities. Others had mental health problems. Some were elderly people, some families who were dysfunctional. From a mother whose second husband did not like her son and consequently would not allow me, or the child, back into the house after a week away, through fear of another marriage break down, to a man who shot his wife dead two weeks after I had visited to advise about benefit entitlement. It was life in all its shades, from the ugly and the menacing to the glad and grateful, but it taught me how to listen, how to build relationships quickly and to respect people as human beings no matter what their circumstances or seeming disadvantages in life.

I once had a ride with a mini bus driver who worked for a charity involved with disabled children. His own daughter suffered from Downs Syndrome. I asked if he found it difficult having a child who required constant care. It was tiring he confessed, but the positives far outweighed the negatives. In particular, his daughter's disability had brought him into contact with a whole range of people he would not have otherwise met, including the Queen. Neither he nor his wife had any regrets. Their daughter had brought them more pleasure than they could have ever imagined.

To celebrate my new job, Angie and I decided to purchase a small hatchback. We were excited at choosing the colour of the body (bright turquoise) and the design of the upholstery and were proud to be the owners of that year's model. We had also planned a special holiday to a small hotel in a remote town called Scourie in Northwest Scotland. Angie had just commenced driving lessons and we felt that it would be mutually beneficial for the driving to be shared.

It was during our second day of travelling up the West coast that a miracle occurred. Driving alongside a loch, during one of the remotest stages of our journey, the driver of a car we had been following suddenly pulled to a halt, in order to appreciate the rugged scenery. Angie had decided to slowly overtake and began to edge past the car as the road was narrow. I have never been a good 'back seat driver' and believing I could execute the operation more skilfully, assisted Angie in turning the steering wheel. My intervention caused her to loose control of the car and seconds later, our brand new, Volkswagen Polo was stuck fast, driver's side down, tightly wedged in a deep rocky ditch that ran alongside the road.

I had landed on top of Angie, but we just managed to push the passenger door open and clamber from the car unhurt. It was obvious though that there was no hope of the car being recovered without substantial assistance. The driver of the car we had avoided offered to take us to the nearest farmhouse, some miles away, in order to phone for a breakdown truck.

Angie agreed to stay on her own with our car until we returned.

Fortunately, the elderly Scottish couple who owned the farmhouse were more than willing to help and suggested I telephoned the garage at Ullapool several miles away. The garage owner made it clear that to retrieve the car would require 'heavy lifting gear' and that he would dispatch the necessary equipment as soon as possible. It was with nervous trepidation that I made the return journey.

Having watched us disappear from view Angie had sat by the roadside and wondered what to do next. We were a long way from home and for the first time in our married life, were without the support of friends and family. There was no way of resolving the situation without a great deal of time, effort and expense. Our precious holiday together was on the brink of being ruined. We were about to discover, however, that when our resources run out, God moves in. That God is a Father who cares for His children. We were about to experience the reality that sometimes God even answers our prayers before we pray them.

Initially the road had been completely empty. However, after a few minutes, a large white van appeared on the horizon. The van drew closer and then drove by. Eventually it stopped a short distance beyond where Angie was sitting and reversed. The van pulled up beside the car and the back doors opened. A number of men jumped out of the van, climbed down into the ditch and positioned themselves around the car. With some effort they lifted the car out of the ditch and placed it back onto the road. They then climbed back into their van and drove off. From start to finish they said hardly a word.

It was with complete disbelief, when I returned some minutes later, to see Angie still sitting by the side of the road alone but grinning, with the car next to her.

With grateful thanks, we tried to start the car, but the accident had caused some damage to the engine. I therefore returned to the farmhouse to cancel the 'heavy lifting gear,' but instead to request a car mechanic be sent as soon as one was available.

Having watched us disappear from view a second time, Angie again sat by the roadside. After a few minutes a car appeared on the horizon. It drew closer and stopped. A young man got out and having announced he was a car mechanic lifted up the bonnet and began to assess the situation. He quickly identified the problem, made the necessary adjustments and started the engine. He then climbed back into his own vehicle and drove off. It was with humble belief when I returned a few minutes later, sat in the driver's seat of our much dented vehicle and drove away.

During the next week we drove over 800 miles. The car did not let us down once.

Whilst on holiday Angie and I visited an ex-army base near Cape Wrath whose buildings had been taken over by a group of artists and craftsmen. In one of the buildings a man was making words and shapes by welding nails together. Some of the words had been fashioned to form a sentence. We purchased one of his creations. It now hangs in our living room. The sentence reads, 'Tell It Like It Is'. Ever since as Christians, we have tried to do just that.

Occasionally, Angie and I would take part in a Craft Fair, held in an old barn in Suffolk. Angie would demonstrate her skills in Batik (a process of creating an abstract design using wax on cotton or silk and then dying the material) that she had learnt at Teacher Training College. I would sit nearby with an Inkle Loom and demonstrate weaving. Art was never my strongest subject at school. My art teacher said that when I drew people they looked like trees, but I found that even though I did not have a clue about how to weave, if I looked confident enough I could make the right impression. Fortunately no one ever asked me to explain the finer details of the craft.

On other weekends we would visit Jack. Jack had been born physically and mentally healthy in every respect. But during his teens, an extreme reaction to the death of his father had caused brain damage that led to him suffering from cerebral palsy. By middle age, he was confined to a wheelchair having weakness and impaired coordination in all his limbs. His speech was barely discernible. Whilst in the sixth form, as part of a community placement, Angie had visited Jack who lived in a specialist residential home. It was fortunate that, despite his severe disability, Jack had retained his sense of humour and fun as, on long walks in the countryside, Angie would often race the wheelchair over rough ground and take corners on two wheels. Once Jack was actually catapulted from the wheelchair. He survived and his beaming smile demonstrated that his virtual experience of being in a two man bob-sleigh had brought moments of happiness and excitement to an otherwise restricted life.

Angie's friendship with Jack continued after she left school and it was my privilege to also spend time with Jack, holding his claw like hand and trying to engage the vibrant person living inside the physical body that imprisoned him. It was a joy to see him laugh and to watch him participate as fully in our practical jokes as any able-bodied person. He visited us at 'Pegtile Cottage' and in later years held our baby Ben gently in his arms.

Jack died when he was in his sixties. During his life, Angie and I had prayed for him and with him. Hopefully we communicated the fact that he gave as much to us as we tried to give to him and that he was no less a person for his disability. We knew God valued him as he was and we respected him for the way he coped with his pain and loss of independence. We do not know whether he died having a faith in God. But if he did, we do know that his broken body will one day be replaced by one that never wears out.

On many levels our married life was now both enriching and enjoyable, however, our church experience was not matching our daily 'Christian' experience. Since marrying, we had regularly attended Angie's home church. It was traditionally Baptist and although people were friendly, it seemed to lack what we were craving for. More spiritual depth, a church that reflected the principles and power of the church in Acts and a church that was willing to take 'holy risks' in faith.

A few years earlier, the teenagers in the church had begun to exercise what are described in the Bible as 'spiritual gifts', particularly 'speaking in tongues'.

The church leaders had been nervous of what was happening and, in their caution, had discouraged those attending from pursuing these expressions of supernatural spiritual life.

This reluctance to consider other styles of church service or encourage those whose Bible teaching may challenge their own beliefs seemed to mark a turning point. Some years later the church closed. It is now a block of offices.

Although unsettled at the church, we were helped greatly at this time by an older Christian couple who lived a few doors away. Tony and Rosemary Smith had spent several years in Africa as missionaries, and through their experiences had found a spiritual awareness that we wished to discover. They were in one sense ordinary people. Tony a teacher in a comprehensive school, Rosemary a physiotherapist in a local NHS hospital. But we had never met a Christian woman like Rosemary. She had a relationship with God that set her apart. She appeared to have a 'hot line' direct to the Father. I have never known, before or since, a more spiritual person, male or female, and have found it a regrettable weakness over the years in many churches, that spiritual gifting given to women is often not fully recognised or utilised.

Since the beginning of our marriage, Angie and I had shared our faith with each other and sought to reach an understanding on issues where we disagreed. Those times of sharing had taught us to respect and learn from the other's point of view, and by the end of 1976 we had reached a convergence in our thinking. In those early days of our marriage, we were learning the principles of Proverbs 27: 17; 'A friendly discussion is as stimulating as the sparks that fly when iron strikes iron'*. It was to stand us in good stead in the years to come.

*The Holy Bible, Living Bible Edition, Kingsway Publications Ltd, 1994.

We were also learning that there is nothing more important in marriage than faithfulness. Looking at the lives of some of our friends we were aware of the consequences of marriage breakdown. Some tried to justify their position and excuse themselves for their part in the failure. But it seemed to us, if you can't trust the person you are sharing a bed with night after night, who can you trust? Secrets separate couples. Nothing undermines a relationship more than distrust. Angie and I were discovering that there is already enough pain in the world. We did not have to add to it by allowing our affections to wander.

In the early part of 1977 Angie and I began to pray seriously about moving house. Although our cottage had originally met all our needs, we did not feel living near a busy road would be suitable for raising a family. We decided to put our property on the market and see what happened. It sold quickly and for some months we rented a house.

A chance conversation with a former work colleague led us to visit a delightfully dilapidated long, low, timber framed, detached Tudor cottage in a small picturesque village, several miles away from where we had been living.

'It'll need a bit of work doing', my work colleague had said. He was right. But the holes in the roof, the damp in the brick floor, the little kitchen tagged on the back with rotting wooden walls, the low oak beam in the living room that gave a clue to the 'real person' by the language people used when they walked into it, and the inglenook fireplace that encouraged smoke to waft into the room rather than up the chimney, did not put us off. We purchased the cottage for £10,000.

The cottage had been called 'Dormers,' but because we had taken up residence in August, we renamed it September Cottage. We have a strange sense of humour.

September Cottage was so old it was like living in a museum. Our Bank Manager had advised us that, 'It had potential', and on that basis agreed to offer us a mortgage to renovate the property. The plans were drawn and the builders, a small two-man company, booked to commence work in the following year.

We were two years into our marriage and ready to take the next step. We were confident that things could only get better. Angie and I were settled in our relationship, were both working full-time, had money to spend and had now discovered the house of our dreams.

The previous owner of September Cottage, a middle aged woman named Peggy Watson, had told us sometimes you can be going along in life and then suddenly, quite unexpectedly you hit a corner and your life changes completely. That had been the case in her own life. She had been quite settled until one day she had met and fallen in love with a man from Zimbabwe. He had turned out to be a member of the government and, now they were married, she was emigrating to Zimbabwe to set up home with him.

Our life to date had been fairly straightforward. But Angie and I were about to discover the truth of Peggy Watson's words. The path ahead would no longer be direct. The 'corners' were already on the horizon.

CHAPTER THREE

The plans for the cottage involved removal of the roof, demolishing the dilapidated rear extension and moving the staircase from the front of the property to the rear.

In early 1978 Angie and I began to undertake some of the demolition work and dig the foundations for the new kitchen, bathroom and toilet. This preparatory labour was physically demanding, and living in a house while it is being taken apart proved to be emotionally draining. There was no escape. We went out to work in the mornings and came back to work in the evenings. It was a case of keeping the bigger vision in our minds whilst living with the day-to-day disruption.

Our two builders, though, proved to be professional and thorough. They were extremely reliable and the work proceeded at a pace. It was not until two months into the build that we encountered a major problem. The builders had invested a lot of their own money in building materials and had so far not been paid for their labour. I had naively assumed that payment would be made on completion of the work. It was apparent, however, that an interim payment would be required to keep the builders financially solvent. I contacted the bank thinking that the matter would be resolved overnight.

Some weeks later a bank official arrived to inspect the work. He was pleased with the progress but did not feel that any payment as yet could be made. This placed the builders in a difficult position. They needed to continue working on our cottage to complete the job, but had outstanding bills to pay and no income. They agreed to take on other jobs to provide themselves with an income and work on our property as and when they could.

The months dragged by. Eventually the renovation was completed, but the situation had led to a serious rift between us and the builders, and as the cost of raw materials over the period had risen, their final invoice far exceeded their original quote.

The 'house of our dreams' had become a financial nightmare. We extended our mortgage and although, with us both working we could just meet the repayments, it left us with little spare cash. We managed to save enough to insert a wood burner in the inglenook fireplace, but could not afford to install central heating in the rest of the property. We filled the house with any second-hand furniture we could find.

In order to reduce our outgoings, we cut back in every area of our lives. We sold our new car and bought one that was second hand. Angie started cycling the six miles to and from work every day. We cancelled all our insurances and stopped buying clothes.

It was fortunate that Angie and I were partial to minced beef. Mince was cheap to buy and versatile. We lived on it for the rest of the year.

Following our move to September Cottage we had begun to look for a new church. There were a number in the area and, without having a preference for any of them, we had begun to attend a Baptist Church in the next village, Sible Hedingham.

The building itself was uninviting; about 200 years old and architecturally elementary. Inside there were wooden pews, at the front a high wooden pulpit and an upstairs gallery which was in considerable need of repair. A year earlier the church had appointed a new minister, George Balfour. He was a Yorkshire man, working for Essex County Council in a senior position, in the Planning Department.

We had never met a church leader like George. When he preached he was to the point and honest. He was able to apply the Bible to subjects that were relevant to everyday living. His Christianity was real and practical. His praying was powerful. When people worshipped God, it was meaningful. I had never been told before that when singing hymns or songs, you were allowed to repeat a verse. It came as a complete revelation. This freedom within the church service allowed the congregation to participate in a way Angie and I had never experienced.

On our first visit George had said to us, 'If you are looking for a church that is comfortable and traditional, then don't come here, go to the church down the road'.

As soon as Angie and I heard those words, we knew we had found what we had been looking for.

One of those involved with the music in the church was Fred. Fred was a talented guitarist and player of the blues harp. I had still not progressed beyond three guitar chords, but I had found a creativity in song writing.

Fred and I combined our talents and began to take assemblies in local schools. Believing ourselves to be at the forefront of contemporary Christian folk music, we wanted a name that was cutting edge, theologically profound and described in a word what we were about. But sometimes originality is hard to come by. Fred and I trawled our imaginations and eventually discovered the perfect title. As my nickname was 'Mogs', we called ourselves 'Frogs'.

It was not long, however, before Fred and I felt the need to develop our musical prowess. We enlisted the help of a keyboard player, a bass guitarist and a drummer. We described our musical style as 'soft rock' which although sounding like the name of a colour on a paint chart, put us, we felt, at the centre of the Christian music scene. To broaden our musical scope, I gave up playing the guitar and wrote lyrics instead. It was a productive partnership. By the end of 1978 we were playing to church audiences across the region. The time commitment for practices was demanding, but for the five of us personally rewarding and a chance to 'serve God' in our own way. 'Salt and Light Company' were on the road.

The winter of 1978/79 was particularly severe. It snowed heavily and was bitterly cold. On one occasion, as no cars could get in or out of our village, a friend from the church loaded his land rover with essential supplies, fought his way through the snow drifts and then shared them with us and the other villagers.

Opposite our home was a hill and during the cold weather Angie and I and our dog Toby would take a sledge up the hill and race each other down the slope. Without proper heating, it was cold inside the cottage. So cold, that one night our hot water bottles froze in the bed! Despite the cold, though, and a precarious financial situation, Angie and I were grateful that we now had a lovely cottage in the country and belonged to a church where God was active in people's lives.

We were settled as a couple and, having discussed our situation at some length, Angie and I decided it would be wise not to have children just yet, in order to place ourselves on a more stable financial footing. Angie was advancing her teaching career, I was progressing in social work and particularly enjoyed the recognition that performing in public with Salt and Light Co was bringing. I was the 'front man' for the band, and as time progressed discovered that there was another side to my personality. In private I was quiet and unassuming. But in front of an audience I changed.

I remember when I was a child, being taken to see my paternal grandfather perform on stage with a friend to a group of older people in Chiswick. The pair of them would sing songs from the period, particularly those of George Formby. They would tell jokes and in time became amateur entertainers. My own father had no interest in performing in public, but that didn't matter. My grandfather had already sown the seed in me.

It was easy for me to commit myself to the weekly practices as Angie and I, apart from work, had few other demands on our time. But that was about to change.

On March 22nd Angie wrote in her diary, 'Rang doctors – test results positive, so pregnant! – staggered, didn't know whether to laugh or cry... pleased really... lovely feeling. I can't wait to tell Mogsy. Cycled home, got caught in hail/sleet storm. Said 'hello Daddy' to

Mogs...who kept saying 'well done' and was very pleased.'

We were thrilled, although nervous of how we would manage. Our relatives were also delighted as it was the first grandchild in both families.

We planned as best we could for Angie to leave teaching in the coming July and sought to deal positively with the reality of our situation. As part of my work involved visiting people in their homes, reliable transport was essential. Our car was frequently unreliable and repair bills were a constant drain on our limited resources. In April a friend from the church sold us at a reduced price a Fiat 500. A tiny car with an engine in the rear. It was like driving an enclosed go-kart. But it started in the mornings and was very economical.

In the comprehensive school where Angie worked, she made a point of building relationships with the children whenever she could. This had resulted in us taking a class of children to stay for a weekend on a barge moored on the mud flats at Tollesbury. The accommodation could only be described as 'basic', but the children, for whom 'real nature' was something your parents watched on television, thoroughly enjoyed a wide range of outdoor activities such as sailing, sea fishing and bird watching.

She had also become particularly close to two lads called Alan and Neville. Both were 'easy going' but in their teenage years their behaviour had drawn them to the attention of the local police. In time, Neville had found himself appearing at Crown Court and had been sent to Hollesley Bay Young Offenders Institution in Suffolk. Angie and I took Neville's mother and sister to visit him. All the lads were dressed in green shirts and black trousers which helped them to become institutionalised very quickly. They had work to do, but for many it proved a useful training ground for a further career in crime.

From time to time Angie had also organised Christian events in the school. On one occasion she had invited two young singer/songwriters to perform at a lunchtime meeting. The hall was packed but some of the children were not in the mood to listen. They talked during the songs and laughed at the Christian content. They dismissed what was going on and encouraged others to do the same. Eventually one of the musicians confronted a small group of boys with the words, 'Do you want a fight? If you do I'll meet you outside in five minutes. If I'm not there by then, start without me!'

Silence reigned for the rest of their concert.

Angie and I were invited to attend a summer wedding in Bridgend. We had no choice but to put our Fiat 500 to its ultimate test. Loaded with a very pregnant wife, a friend's dog, who we were transporting to a new life in Wales and piles of luggage (we would have been good candidates for a Guinness Book of Records award), Angie and I made our way along the M4 to a farm hidden in the hills just above Swansea. The journey, at 45 miles per hour, took several hours and was uncomfortable, but we arrived safely, delivered the dog and next day enjoyed the wedding festivities. Our journey home was no quicker, but fortunately the bumping, shaking, rattling and rolling did not cause Angie to go into premature labour. With the best will in the world, our tiny two-seater could not have been transformed into a mobile maternity unit.

For our fourth wedding anniversary, we took an evening boat trip along the River Stour. Apart from the skipper there were four smartly dressed elderly ladies. When booking, I had chosen the mid-point glass of wine option. I had assumed that everyone on board would be indulging themselves. It turned out, however, that only Angie and I were partaking of the liquid refreshment and we felt extremely guilty when the skipper poured out the wine, watched by the four ladies who made it clear by their expressions they wanted to get on with the voyage. We gulped down the wine. On the return journey we were fortunate not be made to 'walk the plank', for being a little inebriate.

Angie had her first visit from the midwife, Sister Hammond, in October. She was a caring, experienced, self-confident nurse who had a life history that would have made a good novel. She was reassuring and although she preferred to keep the GP's involvement to a minimum, greatly assisted Angie in her preparation for the birth. Angie had been advised that a regular drink of Guinness would be good for her during her pregnancy. Sister Hammond agreed, but also felt red wine would be a helpful companion. She made it clear, however, that our heating needed to be improved straight away. The next few weeks saw the frantic installation of radiators around the house. You didn't argue with Sister Hammond!

Angie had planned to have the baby delivered at our local cottage hospital in Sudbury. At the beginning of November, however, the doctor advised us that as the baby was late it might have to be induced the following week at the West Suffolk Hospital. We were anxious that the baby be delivered naturally, preferably as near to home as possible. Our prayers were answered. On the 16th of November, Benjamin Martin Jones was born at 4.05 pm in St Leonard's Cottage Hospital. The name Ben, means 'Son of my right hand', or 'right hand man'. We did not know it at the time but this little baby would, in the years to come, be a means of strength and support when Angie and I were finding that life was simply not worth living.

Coping with a new baby can be difficult. The practicalities of four hourly feeds, nappy changing, trying to get the baby to sleep and the awesome responsibility of caring for another human being is daunting. Long nights of pacing up and down the bedroom with Ben over my shoulder singing Colonel Hathi's March from the film 'Jungle Book', were a common occurrence.

For the next six months the words, 'Oh we march from here to there and it doesn't matter where, you can here us push through the deepest bush, with a military air, with a military air', haunted me both day and night.

No one had warned us, or if they had, we hadn't listened, of the sudden unexpected loss of freedom and time constraints that a baby places on you. But that was our choice. Children are a gift and we were grateful for this bundle of joy.

New life, though, does not mean old problems disappear. A few days after Ben's birth we had a letter from the Bank advising us that we were overdrawn. Our Fiat 500 was also becoming as unreliable as its predecessor. The village had a very limited bus service and now, as travelling with Ben was akin to moving house, our transport situation became acute. The series of second hand cars and large garage bills that followed did nothing to improve the situation.

It was a tradition in our village for the residents to gather together and go carol singing the week before Christmas. That Christmas they all gathered in front of our cottage and sang 'Away in a Manger.' It was even snowing! Angie and I stood at the front door with Ben, who was mesmerised by the whole experience. We were seriously in debt, but believed, now we were a family, that we could cope with whatever the New Year might bring. But danger signs were already appearing on the path we were walking.

Salt and Light Company were going from strength to strength. The quality of our music was steadily improving and we were now being invited to travel to other parts of the country to play concerts. We began to actively seek a manager and made plans to go into a recording studio as soon as possible. I was driven by the opportunities offered to develop my song writing, being part of a team, the praise of the audiences and the freedom from parenting. The evening band practices were demanding, but provided a justifiable means of avoiding my responsibilities as a father and husband. Serving God is always a sacrifice for somebody.

I decided that if I was to make an impact on stage, image was important. Looking right enhanced your status. I needed some professional advice. Angie had an old school friend, who worked for two men who owned a clothing shop in Colchester. David and John had a business acumen that was second to none. If it was in fashion, it was in their shop. With their patient help and advice, I purchased some clothes that were not only fashionable, but a statement of good design. David and John were homosexuals, a lifestyle I could not condone, but they were two of the nicest men I have ever met.

Band practices were not the only call on my time. The church was also growing and as a consequence George was finding it difficult to cope with the work load. In February, along with Tony Smith, I became a part of the leadership team.

On Sunday mornings, before the service, all the leaders would pray in a room behind the pulpit. When everyone in the congregation was seated we would process into the church. It made my day. I was proud to be a leader and wanted everyone to know.

I was not aware of the impact my absences from the home were having on Angie and our relationship. For her, every day was centred on caring for Ben, undertaking household chores or pushing a buggy aimlessly around the village. It was true, Angie was thrilled to see Ben suck his thumb for the first time, start on solid food, manage eye-to-hand coordination, roll himself over, first word, first tooth, first laugh, but there was another side of her that was trapped inside the house. Angie had taken up offers of teaching on odd days, in order to improve our finances, but this had meant 'farming' Ben out to friends or relatives, which had proved to be unsettling for him. Angie could have returned to work, but we were uncomfortable with the idea of having a child and then handing him over to someone else to parent. Once passed, those first years are lost forever. Angie was enjoying being a mother but was missing my company and feeling excluded from everything I was involved in. But we did not talk about our situation. How could we? I was never at home.

Early in the year we were advised by our bank manager to sell the house and try and repay some of our debts. But we were not prepared to move. The house was all we had ever wanted. Instead, I began looking for a job with a better salary and Angie started keeping free range chickens to provide us with 'free' eggs.

In May, a Dedication service for Ben was held at Sible Hedingham Baptist Church. It did not mean that Ben became a member of the church, but that as parents we were publicly thanking God for giving him to us and committing ourselves to raising him in line with our Christian beliefs.

What I did not know on that day was that Angie was already two months pregnant with a baby girl. God and wives are full of surprises!

As Ben grew into 1981 Angie began looking for a baby sitter to allow her some free time. She found in the village a teenage girl named Trina Martin who was willing to look after Ben on occasional evenings. We did not know many famous people and were therefore pleased to discover that Trina's father John was the Chief Dalek in the BBC series Doctor Who. Toddlers, however, are no respecter of persons and Ben was as mischievous with Trina as he was with anyone else.

It was with some trepidation that we welcomed Sister Hammond back into our home, but this time the relationship developed into more of a friendship. We shared the preparations and all became more relaxed in the process.

Emily Elizabeth Patience Jones was born in St Leonard's Cottage Hospital on the morning of March 14th. Emily was two weeks overdue but when the birth came it was quick. The labour pains had started at 5am and by 7am Emily was being cradled in her mothers arms. She was perfect. Mother and daughter returned home two days later. We were complete. We now had a 'pigeon pair'. As a couple it was more than we could have hoped for, or had prayed for.

Although we had made every effort to clear our monthly overdraft, by August it had become clear that we were simply living beyond our means. We had thought a credit card might help by allowing us to purchase items and delay paying for them. But our self discipline was no match for the lure of consumerism. We found that having a credit card only encouraged us to buy things we could not really afford, nor often really needed. We decided to ceremonially cut it into pieces. We have never had one since.

We reluctantly began to consider what other properties might be available for us to purchase. One of the estate agents we contacted showed us the details of a property situated in a quiet no-through road called Rosemary Lane which led to the hamlet of Rushley Green, near the village of Castle Hedingham.

It was a smallholding that included a two hundred year old farmhouse, 'Rosemary Farm' and two acres. In addition there was a large barn and outbuildings. Our hopes soared in the expectation that God was leading us to somewhere even better. We put in an offer straight away. But the offer was rejected.

In October Emily's dedication service was held at Sible Hedingham Baptist Church. It was to be a turning point. We finally decided to sell September Cottage to resolve our financial problems, but there was also one more decision that I had to make.

I knew that although Salt and Light Company were on the verge of success my family and my relationship with Angie had to come first. The band played its final concert in Sheringham, Norfolk in December.

As the New Year began, Angie and I began house hunting and seeking a prospective buyer. The latter proved easy. It was not long before a purchaser was found and the necessary paperwork completed. But our house hunting was protracted. When it came to finding a home for ourselves Angie and I were choosy. We wanted our children to enjoy the peace and tranquillity of country living and we wanted a house with character.

We were therefore delighted when an older property became available on the outskirts of Sible Hedingham. It had a beautiful garden that backed onto woodland and a river. The young couple who were selling seemed to like us and accepted our offer without hesitation. We were settled at last and prepared to move.

As the days progressed, however, I became increasingly uncertain that we had made the right choice. Angie and I had always worked together when making decisions, but this time, against all reason, there seemed to be something inside me saying we should not buy the house. I did not want Angie to be disappointed and to place us, as a family, in a situation where we could be potentially homeless, but the feeling would not go away.

With Angie's reluctant agreement I phoned the vendors. They were very upset, Angie was very embarrassed and we returned to square one. Angie and I reconsidered our position. A modern semi-detached property had become available near the church. It was situated on a busy road but required no maintenance. As the church was now beginning to make an impact on the area, we wondered if God wanted us at the heart of the community. Free to follow any of the new

MAURICE JONES

avenues of church work that were beginning to emerge. We agreed to set aside our own feelings and buy the house.

Some days later we decided to walk past Rosemary Farm and contemplate what might have been. The property had now been purchased by an antique dealer from Grays, called Garry who wanted to use the barn to store furniture. We carried on walking. The next house was called Arden Cottage. Although in a lovely position bordered by a wood on one side and a field on the other, the property was in a poor state of repair and the garden overgrown with stinging nettles. It was an ugly house, with no upstairs windows at the front. It was like a child's drawing.

'Who in their right mind would want to live there?' we commented.

We carried on walking. A little further on was an oak beamed cottage, with a large garden. It was like a something from a picture book. We had already come to terms with living in a modern house but agreed that I should ring the farmer who owned the cottage, just in case it was for sale. The farmer advised me that he was not selling the property I was enquiring about, but that he did have another house in Rosemary Lane that he was about to put on the market. It was called Arden Cottage.

We moved into Rosemary Lane in July. Arden Cottage would require substantial renovation, but the location more than compensated for that.

Our second hand cars were still a continual cause of irritation, but generally our finances were at last on a secure footing. We now had it all. A new home, two beautiful children and a strong marriage. But more than that, I had at last begun to grow up. To become a man rather than an adolescent masquerading as one.

I had finally put away my 'boys toys'. Finally realised that, although escapism releases you from the real world, it can also trap you in the land of egocentricity.

CHAPTER FOUR

Sible Hedingham Baptist Church was gaining a reputation for itself. Numerical growth continued during the second half of 1982, although mainly at the expense of other churches in the surrounding area. George's preaching was dynamic, the music led you into a sense of God's presence and there was evidence that the Holy Spirit was touching people's lives supernaturally.

People were healed both physically and emotionally in ways that could not be explained by reason or self-healing. Not everyone was healed when prayed for, but lives were changed for the good.

'Praying in tongues' was evident in most meetings, sometimes 'singing in tongues' when many people in the congregation sang in harmony in a strange language. It was not rehearsed, nor organised, it just happened spontaneously. And it was beautiful. There was no pressure from the leaders to manipulate the meetings. Christianity suddenly became exciting!

On occasions, people wanting prayer would line up at the front of the church. Often, when George prayed for them, they would fall backwards and be semi-conscious for a few minutes. In order to prevent people hurting themselves when they fell, those of us in leadership, were asked to stand behind and catch them. For some reason, although not known for an outstanding physique, I was often asked to stand behind ladies who were rather on the large size. It had to be the power of the Holy Spirit that moved them. A push or some other artificial means of propulsion would have had no effect whatsoever!

Baptismal services often took place and attracted large congregations. Those attending the church demonstrated a real care for others and were genuinely interested when people inside and outside the church faced difficulties.

The church was attracting young and old alike and weekly activities increased to meet the demand. Because of my social work experience I was asked to lead a counselling team and train members of the congregation to be competent when people asked for their help. I now also had the opportunity to lead services and occasionally speak. Again, it was a pleasurable experience for me to be in front of an audience but I was learning that seeking to lead adults closer to God was not like putting on a performance. If people were giving up their time to listen to you, it was important to have something worthwhile to say. Also, to be credible, a leader needed to actually practice what they preached. To lead by example. Sometimes, though, it was an uphill struggle. Young children have a knack of knocking people off their self-made pedestals. One Sunday, during the morning service, Ben said loudly, 'Don't pick your nose daddy', and a few weeks later as two ladies finished singing a duet, he said even more loudly, 'What are you laughing at daddy?'

Our leaders' meetings were always lively. We were learning to work as a team and that involved not only expressing our individual opinions, but also listening to what others had to say. There was an expectation that our discussions should be frank but fruitful. We were not looking for compromise, we were trying to find God's will for the way ahead.

The only negative within the church was an adherence to gender separation. Although it was quite apparent that God was giving spiritual gifts to both women and men and that women were able to hold high profile positions in the children's work and prayed powerfully, often Men's meetings or Women's meetings were organised to promote that particular group's spiritual enhancement. Often, though, the opposite was true. The meetings tended to promote unequal spiritual growth, particularly amongst married couples and encouraged the discussion of issues from a one-sided perspective.

Whenever possible, which was most of the time, Angie and I avoided them.

At the beginning of her diary for 1983, Angie wrote, 'Mogs is thirty!...applying for grants for cottage/digging garden etc/launching counselling course at church.

I'm 28...teaching 2hrs a week, fighting to start a –playgroup...mostly at home with little 'uns. Ben 3, Emily $1^{3/4}$... Ben-enjoying riding his new bike – likes helping Mogs – plays imaginative games-(talks to his toys etc) loves joining in at crèche – with songs, rhymes etc. – annoyed sometimes by Emy-but generally very caring for her. Emy-tries to say most things – manages sentences sometimes, eats non-stop, always demanding food or drink – loves a cuddle and hugs, very affectionate and cheeky.'

One of the drawbacks of moving to Rosemary Lane was that there seemed to be few children of Ben's age. There were a handful of houses in the lane and most were occupied by those who were elderly, or without children.

We were delighted therefore to discover that a short distance from our home was a young couple, who had a son named Matthew. He was one month older than Ben. For Angie and I it was an answer to prayer. It was reassuring to know that God was interested in even the smallest details of our lives. Over the years Matthew and Ben have been able to share schools and much of their lives together. Matthew remains one of Ben's closest friends.

During the previous year Angie and I, along with another couple, had been asked to take on the running of a house group. A small group mid-week meeting of church members with time to share the Bible and their lives together. But being in a small group enabled us to develop areas other than prayer and Bible study. In January we put on a pantomime, 'Cinderella', to the whole church. We had written the script between us, but were not sure what level people's acting ability would reach. We needn't have worried. Those in the group who were often the quietest and seemingly austere came to life when given the opportunity to take part in an amateur production.

Angie and I also wanted to take part in the performance but keep a low profile.

The solution was easy. We hired a pantomime horse costume and pulled Cinderella's coach. Not to be left out of the action, Ben broke loose from his 'minder' and joined us on stage. Our six-legged pantomime horse brought the house down!

After some months of trying, we received a grant from the council to improve Arden Cottage. Although the renovations were again extensive, this time the money was available to pay the builder as required. Having a larger garden, Angie was keen to enlarge her flock of free range hens. A friend's brother owned a battery farm some miles away and he agreed to let us have some of his one year old hens, as by that age, he told us, they were past their best.

We had never been inside a battery farm. Seeing hundreds of chickens in metal cages, living in artificial light, pecking the feathers out of each other until they were bald, took our breath away. They may have been protected from the weather and illness, but they had in essence simply become egg-laying machines.

The chickens we bought, although they had never seen bare earth, were soon scratching in the soil. They may have never experienced the warmth of the sun, or fresh air, but amazingly their natural instincts were still intact. Their egg output continued for at least another two years. It seemed to us that farming chickens on an industrial scale may provide cheap food, but keeping them in inhumane conditions demeaned human beings.

For some time Angie had been concerned that in Sible Hedingham there was little provision for pre-school children. The church building had now been refurbished and all the pews removed. A Mother and Toddlers group was already running and Angie, along with another friend from the church, started a playgroup.

From the beginning they had decided it was important the playgroup set itself high standards of equipment and activity. They felt it honoured God if everything was done to the highest possible standard. Their formula worked. The playgroup soon established itself as one of the best in the area and the church established itself as part of the local community.

To circumvent the danger of church work becoming all consuming, Angie began playing for a local ladies' netball team and I recommenced writing. This time, though, not songs but children's stories. Whilst at secondary school in Hounslow I had started to write poetry to express my feelings and confusions. In the sixth form at Bognor Regis Comprehensive while studying for an A level in English, I had been encouraged to write in a variety of styles. This had culminated in the penning of a play which I proudly entitled 'The Seagull', having spied the bird while looking for inspiration out of the library window. I had yet to discover that a rather more famous play than mine had already been given that title.

Having young children brought me into contact with children's literature. I enjoyed using my imagination and playing with words and sounds in order to create a picture on a page. After some months, *I'm Going on a Dragon Hunt* was completed and I began to send the story to various children's publishers. It was to be a long, slow process and several times I had to rewrite my 'masterpiece'. But I learnt that perseverance can eventually bring rewards.

With our house renovations complete Angie and I were feeling the need for a holiday. Angie had discovered a three bedroom holiday flat attached to a working farm near Peasenhall, Suffolk and we booked in for a week at the beginning of October.

The flat was warm and spacious with an upstairs lounge that looked out over the farm. Gus and Mary, the owners, were very welcoming and allowed us to wander freely. In the mornings, their umpteen dogs would race up our stairs and jump on the beds. If we were asleep the dogs licked you until you opened both your eyes!

During our stay Gus gave Ben and Emily a ride around the farm in his pony and trap and gave me the opportunity to help him feed his pigs. I had never been that close to a live pork sausage. Like most people, I did not think about where the meat I ate actually came from when I picked up a ready wrapped joint from the supermarket shelf. I was only interested in the product, not its source. The animals, although constantly hungry, had real personality and you could see in their eyes a blissful look when you scratched the tough skin on their backs. It did

MAURICE JONES

not put me off eating meat but increased my interest in animal welfare. One of Gus and Mary's dogs, a Jack Russell, was about to give birth. We could not prevent ourselves from ordering a puppy which, when we finally brought it home, we called Gussey in honour of our host! During the following year we were to stay at the farm on a number of occasions. It gave us the space to spend time together as a family and offered solitude and escape. We made good use of the time we had together. I'm glad we did. We never realised the devastation that lay ahead.

A few days before Easter 1984 I received a phone call from my brother to tell me my father had died following a heart attack. He was 59. I was stunned by the news. My father had always been there. Always ready to offer help and advice. He had been a quiet man, but had also had a comic side to his personality. This, though, had been tarnished by the bitterness of the Post Office strike in 1971, when he, along with work colleagues, had taken strike action, without pay, for seven weeks. The strike had achieved nothing and my father, for the remaining years of his life, was never quite as humorous.

He had become a Christian at a Billy Graham Crusade so the funeral was tinged with joy. But filling the gap left by the death of someone you love is impossible. And the pain extreme.

I refocused on my writing. A Christian friend, John Prothero, who was an able musician, and I began to write songs around the Bible story of the Prodigal Son. We were fortunate to have in the church a drama teacher who was able to write some dialogue and give the whole project a structure. George had suggested that the church could benefit from working together by publicly performing the material John and I were writing. Rehearsals for 'Fly Away Peter' began in earnest that autumn with George playing the part of the Prodigal Son's father.

But that was not George's only commitment. He was now being invited to preach outside the church and was also invited to speak to churches in South Africa. He accepted the invitation and arranged to fly out to Johannesburg at the beginning of September the following year. That autumn, Ben commenced his education at the local primary school in Castle Hedingham. Angie would walk Ben to school through the fields.

He and Emily could run down Scotch Pasture, a nearby meadow, and roll in the grass. Make daisy chains. Moo at the cows. It was perfect for children.

'Fly Away Peter' was performed in Sible Hedingham comprehensive school in the spring of 1985 to packed audiences on three nights. The preparation had been time consuming and demanding, but the combination of a wide variety of talents within the church had enabled a production of some quality to be presented to the public at large.

I also received confirmation from André Deutsch, a London publisher, that they liked *I'm Going on a Dragon Hunt*, and wished to proceed with publication. For Angie, she was feeling the need to re-establish her teaching career and returned to teaching on a part-time basis.

Because of church growth we, as a leadership team, agreed that some of the groups that were meeting midweek in various houses which were situated outside of Sible Hedingham, should become churches in their own right and serve their own particular locality. Angie and I were given responsibility to establish a new church plant in Great Cornard near Sudbury, and in preparation for its launch in the autumn attended the local house group in Great Waldingfield. Neither Angie nor myself had had any formal training in running a church, but we were confident that given our combined talents and the enthusiasm of the group, we could establish a church that would have a positive impact on the neighbourhood.

Angie and I were also now becoming confident enough to leave Ben and Emily with friends or family while we spent time together. This had culminated in us spending a night in a hotel in London, having first enjoyed a performance of 'The Mousetrap'. When we arrived at the hotel, the receptionist had said she was going to upgrade our room. Completely taken aback we asked why? Smiling, the receptionist said quietly, 'Because you're nice'.

We were initially embarrassed, but had to conclude that hotel receptionists must have a lot of insight!

Best of all, though, we enjoyed being together as a family, and that summer we decided to treat ourselves to a special holiday. We had never visited the Channel Islands but had been advised that they offered sun, sand and scenery. Being adventurous we booked a week in a self-catering cottage on the island of Sark. The advice we had received had not been misplaced. We became completely enveloped in the peace and tranquillity offered by that unique place. The sun shone every day and, with little commercialism and few attractions, we had no other option than to simply spend time together. We didn't mind. It was a holiday to remember and cemented our family relationships even more closely.

Emily was looking forward to starting school, but before the autumn really set in we thought it would be nice to have just one more visit to what Ben and Emily now affectionately called our 'holiday farm'. We booked the cottage for a few days commencing on September 26th.

When the day came we packed our cases, loaded the car and set off in high expectation. The weather was warm and sunny and it seemed to bode well for another few special days together. Just before we left Emily had smiled broadly at me from the top of the stairs. It was one of those precious parent/child, father/daughter moments. It melted my heart. But it was to be her last smile to me before she died.

The year had started with so much promise, but now Angie, Ben and I approached Christmas as three individuals whose present and future seemed to be in ruins. Many of our friends from Castle Hedingham, our church and sometimes even complete strangers who knew of our situation, had all offered us a great deal of love and support during those first difficult months. But, at the end of the day, when the front door was closed and Angie and I held each other tight and cried and cried and cried, we knew we were walking a path along which no one else could come.

Following the accident Angie and I had never really doubted that moments after she had physically died, Emily was in the presence of God. She was safe and secure. What was harder to come to terms with, however, was the pain and desolation of bereavement and trying to adapt to life as a threesome. One of the hardest things after her death was watching Ben wander round the garden without his playmate. We felt like a three-legged dog, incomplete. When it came to Ben's birthday in November, we decided that we would try and make it special for him. We invited all his usual friends and included Katie, Emily's special friend, in the hope that she would provide a link with the past. We gave all the children a torch and let them race around the dark garden.

But all the time we missed the presence of Emily and were glad when the evening was over.

Angie and Ben recovered from their physical injuries quite rapidly and were able to return to a more regular routine within a few months. I, however, still had my right leg in plaster and was therefore confined to spending long periods at home alone.

It was a time of make or break for my Christian faith. I still believed in God, but if He was in control of the world, why couldn't He have averted the accident. Didn't Angie and I as Christians deserve better than this? How could a loving God allow such a thing? Or were we being punished for past misdeeds?

As my leg healed during the Spring of 1986, so I was to embark on ever longer walks through the countryside surrounding our home. It was during these times of solitude that God appeared to be communicating with me in a way that I had not previously experienced. A thought would come into my mind. I would remember a conversation or Bible verse that would seem to meet exactly my need for that day. During those walks, a deep sense of His presence became a regular occurrence, almost as if Jesus himself were walking alongside me. In the quietness, in the brokenness of my life, in the desperation of it all, I did not feel alone. The sceptic might laugh. The atheist might mock. My grief may have been playing tricks with my mind. But it did not feel like that. Somebody was there. Somebody had their hand on my shoulder. Every day I poured out to Him everything that was troubling me, and found I had an attentive, sympathetic listener. God's reply, though, was not what I had expected.

It gradually became clear that, although God loved His children, He sometimes allowed difficult times to come their way, partly to prove their love for Him, partly to teach them something through the experience and partly to help them understand the pain and suffering endured by many every day.

But more specifically, God shared that He was planning to revive His church, by uniting its members. This worldwide revival would be likened to Joshua leading the Israelites into the Promised Land in that whilst there would be spiritual battles along the way, the Christian church would then experience a period of unparalleled growth.

This growth would impact society at every level.

I listened intently to what I believed God was saying, but I also wanted Emily back, and as a consequence prayed fervently for her to be raised from the dead.

I eventually returned to social work and at every opportunity shared publicly that one day God was going to revive His church. But there was one thing I did not quite understand. Four of our closest friends had after the accident written down in a small book some verses from the Bible that they thought would be of comfort to us. We were grateful, but the first two verses they had written in the book did not seem to fit our situation. They were from Habakkuk chapter 2.

> *2And the Lord said to me, "Write my answer on a hoarding, large and clear, so that anyone can read it at a glance and rush to tell the others.*
> *3But these things I plan won't happen right away. Slowly, steadily, surely, the time approaches when the vision will be fulfilled. If it seems slow, do not despair, for these things will surely come to pass. Just be patient! They will not be overdue a single day!"* ★

The verses troubled me. They would not go away.

Months passed, and as each anniversary became less painful, Angie, Ben and I discovered that life could still go on despite all that had happened

---

★*The Holy Bible*, Living Bible Edition, Kingsway Publications Ltd, 1994).

to us. We began to live in the knowledge that although the scars would remain forever, time was healing the wounds.

Although it deeply saddened Angie and I to watch Ben playing on his own, he gradually adapted to being an only child and, as he grew older, began to share some of our interests. The school holidays proved to be the most difficult times to fill and we often booked a two night 'Bargain Break' for the three of us, in London or another city. We found that if worked at, three need not be a crowd and after some consideration, Angie and I decided not to have any more children. Coupled with this decision, I felt that God was now asking me not to speak further about revival. Instead, I began to make notes about what changes might occur in the Christian church if revival came and how that might impact wider society.

The inquest into Emily's death was held at the Coroner's Court in Bury St Edmunds. It appeared that the lorry driver had been speeding and in a moment of panic after the accident had removed his tachograph. The Police had prosecuted him and he had lost his job. Although not deliberate, his moment of indiscretion had cost the life of our daughter. It was easy to be angry with him. But I knew in my heart that bitterness destroys you from the inside and resolves nothing. As we walked from the Coroner's office after the Inquest, I placed my arm around his shoulder and said, 'Don't worry, it's okay'.

With the compensation we received from the accident we were able to buy a brand new car. But our perspective on life was now different. The car meant nothing to us. Acquiring consumer items was no longer important. All the cars in the world could not replace Emily.

We determined to make the most of everyday and to concentrate on building and maintaining relationships with people, not to spend the rest of our lives earning to own. On their deathbed people are not interested in the level of their final salary they want to know they are loved by their family and friends.

On his return from South Africa, George had picked up the reigns of the church again, but it was to only be for a temporary period. He felt his work at Sible Hedingham was now complete and that God was asking him to take up the challenge on a full time basis of working with churches in South Africa.

Having now planted three other churches, Sible Hedingham Baptist Church had become the centre of a large organisation. Roy, one of the leaders, took over the role of Senior Pastor and I, now another leader, was responsible for the church plant in Great Cornard, became a 'roving preacher' with responsibility for teaching in all our different church congregations.

As the leadership team was now divided between the different groups and communication was harder, I was asked to organise a weekend away for the leaders and their wives. Leading leaders is an honour and the request put me right back in the centre of what was going on. I was proud to be part of a church that was going from strength to strength. I was also advised by my publisher that my second book for children would be published the following year.

But life was not all plain sailing. We had to endure the loss of Gussey, when he was run over outside our home by the man delivering fish. It's surprising how attached you can become to an animal. Gussey had become a member of the family. Not in a human sense, but he was a character in a 'doggy' sense of the word, and we enjoyed his company. We associated him with Emily and our times together at the farm. And now they were both gone.

However, it did seem to Angie, Ben and I that the difficult phase through which we, as a family had been passing was now drawing to a close. We could at last look forward to better times ahead.

Angie discovered she was pregnant for the third time in September 1987. Having made the decision not to increase our family, we were both surprised and confused as to how it could have happened despite taking all the usual precautions. We rejected an offer of an abortion from our GP when we told him it wasn't a planned pregnancy and Angie and I eventually became resigned to the fact that God again had something planned for us that we had not anticipated. After a while, we began to feel that although Emily could not be replaced, another daughter might help to restore something that had been stolen from us.

Simeon Thomas Jones was born at home at 5:15am on 23rd May 1988. Sister Hammond had stayed with Angie throughout the night walking with her up and down Rosemary Lane to speed up the delivery. Sister Hammond managed the whole procedure without assistance and fortunately did not ask me to do anything except hold Angie's hand. Angie wrote in her diary, 'He looks like Ben a little, has Mogsy's legs, feet, bottom and my hands. Nose like a strawberry. Dark hair. Enjoys listening. Weighs 6lb 14oz'.

A few days later Ben, who was now eight years said to him, 'You're a poor little old boy…you don't like being a baby do you?'

Although perhaps initially disappointed that it was not part of God's plan for us to have another daughter, the demands and delights of new life quickly overtook us. We borrowed back most of our baby care equipment and, being older parents, were confident that we would cope well with our new son.

The first few weeks confirmed our optimism. Simeon put on weight, slept well and appeared in all respects to be developing normally. Angie and I were determined from the outset that our baby would fit in with us as a family as far as possible, as we were conscious that Ben could easily be neglected, and we also wished to continue with parts of our former lifestyle. By the start of July Simeon's weight had reached 9lb 6oz and he was already managing to smile.

Simeon's Dedication service was held at Sible Hedingham Baptist Church later that month. Knowing what Simeon's birth had meant to us, the church was full of friends and relatives. Fred led the singing, John Prothero led the service and Roy undertook the dedication ceremony. During that part of the service, Roy gave me the opportunity to pray for Simeon. I thanked God for the gift of new life and prayed that as Simeon grew he would teach us more about God and His Kingdom. I should have known better. God always takes us at our word.

It was at the beginning of August, two days before our holiday, that the health visitor suggested we should make an appointment for Simeon to see our GP. She was not unduly concerned but his weight gain had slowed and he was suffering from a cold. The doctor's insistence therefore that we immediately take Simeon to the children's ward at the West Suffolk Hospital came as a complete surprise. We left the surgery with a sealed envelope to give to the ward staff. When we arrived Simeon's name was already on the door of a single room. Although nursing staff rejected our requests to take Simeon home, we were confident that our visit to the hospital would be brief. We were wrong.

It was four long worrying weeks before Simeon was allowed to leave. On admission to hospital, it was discovered that he was in heart failure as a result of congenital heart disease and could die without immediate medical intervention.

Although Simeon's condition was initially stabilised with medication, numerous x-rays and tests revealed that he would require an operation for correction of a double outlet right ventricle, a complex heart operation.

The memories came flooding back, like an action replay of everything that had happened before. Indeed, Simeon was even on the same ward to which Ben had been admitted after the accident three years earlier. It was with complete bewilderment Angie and I received the news that Simeon would have to be admitted to Guy's Hospital for further investigations. Had we not been faithful to all that God had asked of us? To be taken to the depths of despair twice was almost too much to bear.

Simeon's admission to Guy's Hospital in October confirmed our worst fears. Although major surgery was normally avoided until a child was at least two years of age, to heighten the chances of recovery, Simeon's condition was such that the operation could not be delayed. Angie and I were told that there was a 20% risk of death and also the possibility of brain damage or liver failure. We were warned that if Simeon survived the surgery, the following three days in intensive care would be critical and it might be some months before he returned home. On October 17th Angie and I were asked to come to the hospital to sign the consent forms as the operation was to be performed the following day. The consent forms relieved the hospital of any responsibility should Simeon die. We were told that the surgeon undertaking the surgery had only recently joined the hospital.

His name was Dr Shakeel Qureshi. We did not know it at the time, but Dr Qureshi was one of the world's leading paediatric cardiologists.

Angie and I could not bear to see Simeon go down to the operating theatre the next morning, so we said our goodbyes and returned home. That night we prayed hard. Many of our friends from the church had also been praying that God would heal Simeon's heart so that an operation would not, in fact, be necessary. We too believed that God may work a miracle beforehand. But as the hours ticked by and dawn heralded the arrival of a new day it became clear that it was God's plan for Simeon to undergo the surgery and to work out His purposes through the skills of the medical staff.

A nervous telephone call to the hospital at midday assured us that at least Simeon had come through the operation. The sight that greeted us, however, when we arrived in the intensive care unit some hours later took our breath away. Simeon was completely immersed in tubes and wires, as every bodily function had been taken over by machine. A red scar ran the length of his chest. His hands were tied down to prevent sudden movement. A tube in his throat prevented him from coughing and he couldn't cry as his vocal chords had been damaged. Each of the four children on the ward had an individual nurse who continually monitored every computer reading.

We were told that Simeon was 'holding his own' but that, as yet, there was no guarantee of success. It felt again as if we were on the brink of disaster and that God might not spare us the pain of bereavement a second time. Our prayers for Simeon's healing had all seemed to have gone unanswered.

And then it happened. God moved.

Although it had been anticipated that Simeon would be in intensive care for at least a week, because of his progress he was transferred to the children's ward within six days.

The recovery continued and encouraged medical staff informed us that he may be home for Christmas. On October 27th Dr Qureshi said to Angie, 'Your little boy has been through major heart surgery without batting an eyelid. He can probably go home next week.' Angie had replied, 'But you said he would take up to three months to recover. Dr Qureshi replied, 'Well I got it wrong'.

On the 5th November, just in time for the fireworks, Angie and I brought Simeon home. It was less than three weeks since the operation. God had not forgotten us, but again had posed the question, 'Will you follow me, love me, trust me, even in the darkest moments'.

The events of 1988 had had the potential to destroy our faith, but God had been gracious to us. As we had left the hospital with Simeon, Angie had seen a rainbow in the sky. We knew that the rainbow is God's way of saying there is always hope. We were back on track and life was again on the way up.

CHAPTER FIVE

1989 should have been a year of peaceful progress. The emotional rollercoaster of Simeon's hospitalisation had left Angie and I physically and mentally drained and we were looking for some respite. However, in the next few months, two situations would arise within the church that would culminate in us leaving. The first occurred in January.

Angie and I had always held the view that Christians who divorced should not remarry. We considered that if the promise, 'for better for worse, for richer for poorer, in sickness and in health, till death do us part', had been made to God during the wedding ceremony, that promise should be kept. If a marriage had broken down irretrievably, then God in his grace would allow a couple to divorce. But that was not his preferred option and remarriage simply added insult to injury. Angie and I were advised by Roy that one of the other leaders was planning to marry a divorcee. We were close to both the people involved, but after giving the matter considerable thought, did not feel we could compromise our beliefs.

We discussed our feelings with Roy and agreed to disagree.

Although Roy had overall responsibility of what was now a group of linked churches, each congregation was looking to have its own individual leader. John Prothero was appointed to lead Sible Hedingham Baptist Church.

John and his wife Anne had become two of our closest friends. When

Simeon had been in Guy's Hospital they had arranged a 24 hour prayer vigil. John was physically a tall man, and at our weakest moments, when we needed a 'big' man in every sense of the word to support us, John had been there. His continual encouragement had been a rock to cling to when everything around us was being washed away. We were delighted at his appointment.

The second situation, though, occurred when George returned from South Africa and felt he could be of assistance to John in running the church in Sible Hedingham. Angie and I felt that the church had moved on from when George was leader and that his time had therefore passed. We decided, because of these combined disagreements, that we had no option but to resign our membership after 11 years at the church and for me to step down from the leadership team.

Over the years I have thought long and hard about our decision to leave. Sometimes we make decisions that are right. Sometimes we make decisions that are wrong. Often it is only with the benefit of hindsight that we discover whether the direction we have chosen is the best one. But to live comfortably with ourselves we have to do what we believe to be right at the time and take responsibility for that decision. To condone situations by inertia rarely brings change for the better.

As well as rescuing battery hens, Angie was also concerned about how pigs were often reared indoors without the opportunity to engage their natural instincts. We decided that as we had some space in our garden, we would construct a pig run and try to rear our own. A farmer who lived nearby agreed to sell us two weaners (pigs that are about eight weeks old), which we planned to fatten, then send to the local abattoir for slaughter. We were amazed how clean pigs like to keep their housing and how much they enjoyed digging in the soil. We called them 'Sweet and Sour'. Our biggest difficulty was catching the piglets when they escaped from their run. Small pigs have a good turn of speed and are masters at evading capture. The effort, though, was worthwhile, when in the summer we filled the freezer with enough joints, chops and sausages to last us several months.

We also bought a sow named 'Flossie'. She had a litter of several piglets which we then raised. For a while we thought about expanding into free range pork. Angie even made up a marketing slogan, 'You are what you eat, so eat happy meat. Get your hogs from Mogs'. We decided, though, that our animal husbandry skills were not sufficient for the job and that our idea, like the slogan, would not catch on.

Physically Simeon continued to make good progress, and month by month was achieving all the necessary milestones, although we still had to take him to the West Suffolk Hospital for an annual check up. To celebrate his first birthday, Simeon was featured on the front page of our local newspaper the *Halstead Gazette*, under the headline, 'Special day for miracle baby Simeon'.

Although Angie was enjoying teaching part-time, she was beginning to feel that maybe she should consider a return to full time teaching. In June, Angie was asked if she wanted to take up a full time post at the junior school in Castle Hedingham. She agreed. But as we did not wish to place Simeon with a childminder or send him to a nursery, I agreed to take on the role of househusband. I was about to discover that running a home and creating an environment where everyone, particularly the children, feel valued is one of the most important jobs on earth. Other adults may be able to offer care, but they cannot freely give their time or parental love on a one-to-one basis and children need that more than anything else in the world.

Even though Angie's parents and mine had fulfilled the traditional parenting roles, i.e. the male is the 'bread winner' and the female the housewife, we had never felt within the home, that jobs were gender based. Angie had undertaken most of the cooking simply because she was the better cook. All other jobs we shared. I was a little nervous when Angie left for work that September and I was left at home with Simeon, but the role reversal did not seem unnatural and I looked on it as more of releasing a caged bird. Some of our contemporaries were positive about our change of roles some negative. But we decided it was right for us and did not feel guilty. Philosophically I had to come to terms with the question, 'Was I really a man or was there, hidden deep inside my subconscious, a woman trying to get out?' Now Angie was the 'bread winner' should I still open the door for her? Should I still offer my seat to elderly ladies on the bus? Was it wrong to actually enjoy listening to 'Woman's Hour', albeit with the sound turned down to avoid detection? I knew the answer. I wasn't 'hunky' but I was certain my testosterone was as good as the next man's. Learning to 'multitask' did not have to involve a sex change. Although other people's perceptions of me had changed, I was the same person as before. But this was not a simple job swap. Caring for a home and children requires an emotional as well as a practical investment.

The hardest job was finding the balance between the routine tasks of cooking, washing, ironing and cleaning and the creative task of filling your child's time in a worthwhile manner. That was enough to fill any day. But my responsibilities were not 9 till 5. Often, if Angie needed to prepare lessons or simply relax, running the home went on into the evening. If Simeon or Ben were ill, running the home went on into the night. If I felt unwell, I could not phone up my manager and take a day's sick leave. All leave was cancelled. Caring for a family was rewarding but hard work. The task as important as any other job on the planet. I was saddened, therefore, looking at other families, to see that those who undertook it were frequently undervalued. It seemed that often a person's status was based on their job or salary. Consequently, as a house-husband my worth in the eyes of the outside world, was minimal.

On your own, shopping in a supermarket can be a pleasure. With a small child it can be the height of embarrassment. Replacing items that have been removed by small hands or seeking to pacify a screaming toddler can make you look and feel incompetent as a parent.

It was a lonely job, too. Most social workers are women and I was therefore quite comfortable with having female colleagues. At the local Mother's and Toddler's, though, although I was made welcome, being the only man set me apart. Particularly when it came to conversations about the intimacies of birth from a women's perspective and other conditions peculiar to their body. My childcare therefore became home centred.

During our long hours together, though, Simeon and I developed a close relationship, and no money can buy that.

By March 1990, Simeon was saying, 'Sorry, toilet, seaside, Emily, here's mummy, I love you, where's Ben gone, it's you' when he made a rude noise and 'Hello darling' to the lady in the baker's shop. We knew that one of the valves in his heart was leaking, but generally he seemed to be making good progress. To maintain her relationship with the boys, Angie made a point of reading stories to both Ben and Simeon every night.

At teacher training college in Bognor, Angie had become close friends with two newly married students, Andy and Heather Jones. After completing their training Angie had persuaded them to move to Essex. Andy had progressed as a teacher and by 1990 had been appointed as Head Teacher of a brand new school, named Beckers Green. In March he held interviews for a teaching post with additional responsibilities. He was looking for someone who was caring, had a sense of humour, leadership skills, an ability to form good relationships with people in the community, who valued others and had a willingness to take risks. Over the years Angie's self-confidence in her teaching ability had been undermined by comments from managers that devalued her contribution to the school. The past was about to be put right.

That night we celebrated Angie's appointment with sirloin steak at a local restaurant.

Having left Sible Hedingham Baptist Church, my opportunities for preaching had dried up. Occasionally I would receive a phone call from the leaders of the church plant near Dunmow, asking me to take part in a Sunday morning service. Although my diary was completely blank, for the sake of my ego I would give the impression that although it was difficult, I could possibly squeeze in their request.

Initially on Sundays we attended one of the other church plants near Braintree. We knew many of the people there and fitted in easily. One person we did not know was a young teacher named Elaine. For some years on a voluntary basis, Elaine had been organising an annual 'Beach Club' in Bude, Cornwall for a Christian organisation called Scripture Union. In the summer months these Beach Clubs were held all over the country with the aim of sharing the message of Jesus with children on holiday. The Beach Club was staffed by students who were willing to give up two weeks of their holiday to share their faith. Alongside events for children, there also ran daily Bible teaching sessions for adults. Elaine asked if I was willing to take the adult sessions the following year. I did not need to check my diary. Her timing was perfect. The answer was yes!

That summer, a friend from Sible Hedingham Baptist Church who had moved to France the previous year, invited us to come and stay with him. He had purchased a large stone house in a small hamlet several miles from Limoges. Angie, Ben, Simeon and I travelled by train from Paris and hired a car so that we could stay a few days in his home and then camp on the coast. There were many small farms in the area and we often walked through the surrounding fields and woods. A river ran through a village nearby that offered canoes for hire. At teacher training college, Angie had often canoed up the River Arun and thought it would be nice to give Ben the same experience.

Simeon and I were left to wander through the village for a couple of hours. All the houses had front doors that opened directly onto the street. It was a hot day and the doors were wide open. I could not resist looking in. It was apparent that the lifestyle of the villagers was completely different from ours and that they enjoyed every minute of it. They were French, not Europeans, and they were rightly proud of their individuality, their own culture and their own national customs.

Angie commenced teaching at Beckers Green School in September. Although some of the children were from difficult backgrounds, Angie rose to the challenge. She enjoyed stimulating children whatever their level of intelligence to learn not only from books and computer screens, but from each other and the world around them. Andy wanted children to leave his school not only with a good overall education, but hopefully to also have been set on the path to becoming decent human beings. That aim fitted Angie like a glove. And to some extent it was fulfilled, at least in one life. Carl, because of his physical disabilities would have in years past, been placed in a special school. In a mainstream school he had to take his chances along with everyone else. He needn't have worried. His class mates, instead of ostracizing him, cared for him, helped him, defended him. The school was a richer place because of it.

Angie and I were aware that because of the new demands on our time together, our relationship might suffer if we did not take positive action. We agreed to engage a baby sitter every Thursday night and have a meal in a local pub. We never allowed any other engagement to take its place. We visited the pub so often we became friends of the landlord and his wife. Unfortunately, though, because of a general lack of custom, the pub was eventually sold.

After some months of learning from my mistakes, by March 1991 I was beginning to adapt to my new role at home and beginning to organise myself into a weekly routine. Angie enjoyed cooking at the weekends, and so on Friday night I would hand the house back to her. It was a little complicated at holiday times as neither of us were sure who was responsible for what. Sometimes I would feel 'redundant', but I appreciated that Angie also wanted to contribute to making the home a better place to live. It was a case of us doing the jobs that best suited our talents. During the holidays I continued with the washing and cleaning. I was particularly concerned, if we were having visitors, that the bathroom and toilet were in good order. You can tell a lot about a restaurant or hotel by the cleanliness of their toilets. I took pride in cleaning ours to a high standard every week and before visitors arrived ensured they always had the '5 star' treatment.

I'm not sure anyone ever noticed. If they did they never mentioned it. Cleaning toilets is a humbling experience. It makes you view the world from a different perspective. From the bottom up, so to speak.

I particularly enjoyed taking the washing to the laundrette, when the weather was not warm enough to dry it in the garden. Other people's washing is always more interesting than your own. Opposite the laundrette was a beauty salon, 'Skin Deep'. I would sit and watch the women go in and out. It was apparent that the treatments changed many of the ladies outwardly for the better. But you could see from the looks on their faces afterwards that inside they were still same.

At an outpatients appointment in April at the West Suffolk Hospital, Dr Quereshi advised us that as Simeon was making such good progress he would not need to return to the hospital for another 18 months. He was developing normally in every area. His eye/hand coordination was particularly good.

Although Angie and I had initially thought we could become a part of the Braintree church plant, it became apparent after talking to the leadership that there were a number of matters relating to church membership on which we would have to agree to disagree. In May we began attending a Baptist Church in Sudbury. It was a traditional building, with a traditional style of service, but the minister was welcoming and fatherly to us. There were also a large number of young people attending and Simeon and Ben were able to take part in a number of activities.

At the end of July we travelled to Bude to take part in the Beach Club. The accommodation was basic, dormitories in a private school, but working with a group of Christian students from all backgrounds and all parts of the country was exhilarating.

There was never a dull moment! And there was, in those young people, a spiritual depth that gave them a maturity beyond their years. There were a wide variety of adults in our group. From solicitors to those serving in the armed forces. From people on holiday to serving church ministers. Many had been to the teaching sessions for several years. They were challenging meetings, particularly as the previous leader had adopted a style with which people had become familiar and comfortable. Angie and I had to work hard to encourage people to build on what had gone before, but also to progress into what God was doing in the present.

Angie and I were unfamiliar with some of the traditions of 'Beach Clubs'. One was that all team members had to wear blue tee shirts, and secondly, they had to spend time in the High Street handing out Christian literature. Neither tradition appealed to us. We made sure we kept our coats on over our tee shirts and if we could not avoid walking in the High Street, made sure we crossed over the road if we saw a blue tee shirt up ahead. We were happy to share our faith, but felt it was better to build relationships with people first, so that they trusted you and were therefore more willing to listen to what you had to say. Over the next five years, the Beach Club was to become a regular part of our summer holidays. As a family we received far more from the team than we ever gave. And we learnt a valuable lesson. Working in unity is not only good for those on the inside. Working together means goals can be achieved that benefit everyone.

As it was now six years since the accident and since we had last visited our 'holiday farm', Angie and I felt that it was a loose end we needed to tie up. At the end of August we made our way back to Peasenhall and during the week said our goodbyes to the farm and Gus and Mary. It was the end of a one chapter in our lives and the beginning of a new one. Ben was growing up. In September he started at the comprehensive school in Sible Hedingham. It was to be a partnership that would lead him through A levels, to Leicester University and on to a degree in Geography.

Apart from her teaching responsibilities at the school, Angie was expected to encourage links with the rest of the community. The school was built on a new estate. As there was no community centre the estate lacked a heart. Angie felt it would be beneficial to start a luncheon club for older people, and in September invited several older people to the school for a meal. Some were grandparents of children already at the school, others people living on their own. As well as having a meal, the visitors were entertained after lunch by some of the older children with whom they played board games. As word spread, the luncheon club grew and developed. When the school had special occasions, the older people were also invited.

The luncheon club helped to build bonds between sections of the community and proved to be a positive experience for child and older person alike.

Because of the dark November nights, whatever we had arranged for Ben's birthday always had to be held indoors. Ben and his friends wanted to try something different. I invented a game we called 'Blow out the candle'. A lighted candle was placed on top of a step ladder in the middle of the garden and while Angie and I defended the candle, Ben and the others would try and get to the candle and blow it out. The game proved popular. So popular, as Ben and Simeon grew up we played the game whenever we had the opportunity. With the young and the not so young. It was a game for all ages. It was a game whose impact on our lives would be significant.

In the nativity play at the Baptist Church that Christmas, Simeon was asked to play the part of Joseph. It was a moment that filled us with pride. Simeon had made good progress during the year. But he already knew he was not like other children. When seeing his baby cousin for the first time, he posed the question, 'Why was my heart broken when I was a baby?'

That year during the Easter holidays we attended 'Spring Harvest', a non-denominational annual Christian Bible Week held at the Butlins site in Skegness. The weather was cold and windy which meant that to survive the meetings held in large marquees you had to wrap up warm and keep your umbrella handy! As part of the package all the rides on the funfair were free. There was only one ride we ever used. The bumper cars were made for us. We always had three cars and if we couldn't force each other into the crash barrier we would try and affect carnage on other unsuspecting holiday makers. Fortunately people were too nice to complain.

I always enjoy listening to other people's conversations. While waiting in the queue in the cafeteria one day I stood behind two ladies who helped at the meetings. They were talking about the service the night before. One said that when the speaker had prayed for people at the end, she knew what their problems were before they told her.

Although playing football regularly, it was Ben's tennis skills that were really beginning to develop. He was now having special coaching at the weekends and playing in tournaments around the local area. Every year in July at the tennis club in Castle Hedingham, a tournament for the Junior Singles Trophy was arranged. Ben managed to get through to the final and won two sets to love. He went on to win the trophy three years in a row, a feat never before achieved.

A friend of ours, Lyn, had set up a nursery school in a classroom attached to the primary school in Castle Hedingham. As part of his preparation for full time education, Angie and I enrolled Simeon in the nursery school in September. He made good progress throughout the term. We were not sure at the beginning whether we had made the right decision. When asked by Angie on his first day what he had done at nursery school, the reply had been, 'I did two rudies!'

But Simeon's quick wittedness did not stop there. A few days later when I had asked him to do something, he had looked me in the eye and said, 'What's the magic word?'

Because of Emily's death, Angie and I felt it might be helpful if Simeon were able to attend Beckers Green School with Angie. By so doing, she would not only have the opportunity to spend more time with him on the journey, but watch him grow and develop. Emily's death had taught us that a life can be brief. Angie wanted to spend as much time with Simeon as humanly possible. As we lived outside of the catchment area we had to gain special permission from the Local Education Authority. Permission was granted and Simeon enrolled at the school to start the following year.

Although we got on well with all our neighbours, Angie and I were aware that we rarely met each other on a social basis. In January 1993 we decided to have an 'open house' and invite everyone in Rosemary Lane. Most of our neighbours came. It was a great success. So successful in fact, that in the years since, each neighbour has taken it in turns to host the event with everyone contributing food or drink. Those neighbours who attend are known as the 'Rushley Greenies'. One year we played a game of charades. It's surprising what you find out about people when they are relaxed and not self conscious. Duncan, a farmer living nearby, who was generally shy and unassuming, acted out the most realistic Superman impression I have ever seen.

Angie and I were aware that because Simeon did not attend the school in Castle Hedingham, this might limit his choice of friends. We again though felt it was an answer to prayer that Duncan's son, Andy, was only one year older than Simeon, and in time they became close companions.

Angie was asked to organise the Junior Tennis Club in Castle Hedingham. Ben was now playing regularly and Simeon had just commenced playing short tennis in Sudbury. Although Angie and I didn't play ourselves, we wanted to contribute to the life of the wider community and she therefore agreed.

Simeon commenced at Beckers Green School in April. The first impact school was to have on Simeon was that the following day he demonstrated he had leant to whistle! To begin with it was for mornings only, but he quickly made friends and also grew in self-confidence. Two weeks after starting, while Andy Jones was reading Simeon's class a story, Simeon who was sitting at the front of the group, secretly tied his shoe laces together. I blame the parents!

Angie had often said she would like the experience of flying in a small plane. Not wanting her to be disappointed, I arranged for her to have a flying lesson on her birthday. On our way over to Angie's parents house we suddenly turned off the road and headed for the airfield. She had no time to panic. We stopped by the aircraft and the pilot welcomed her on board. She enjoyed the flight, but vowed to get her own back.

Sometimes it's hard to explain words or concepts to young children. One day Simeon asked Angie, 'What is mercy?' Angie tried to explain. 'Is it like when I had my heart mended', he said. Angie replied, 'Yes, Sim − that's mercy'.

One of the effects of Emily's death was to bring into focus the pain that many people suffer during life. One particular group of people that touched us were terminally ill children and their families. Angie and I had never supported abortion or euthanasia, but we had not been sure how those with terminal illnesses should be cared for. We had begun to financially support the work of a Children's Hospice near Cambridge and in October, were invited to attend an open evening. The work of the staff humbled us. They enabled children to die with dignity and reduced physical pain, whilst offering as much long term support as the families needed. We felt privileged to be a small part of the work.

I had always enjoyed the theatre and in December as a Christmas present, Angie, Ben, Simeon and I travelled to the London Palladium to see *Joseph and His Amazing Technicolor Dreamcoat*. The singing and visual effects were stunning. We did not know it at the time, but a seed had been sown in Simeon's imagination.

Ben's baptism by immersion at the Baptist Church in May was a special occasion for him and us. As Christian parents Angie and I had sought to bring our children up in a way that reflected our faith, but we had tried hard not to force our beliefs on them. It was clear from what Ben said in the service that the decision to be baptised was his and his alone. It was a reflection of his own personal Christian faith. It was the start of a new phase in Ben's Christian life and also in the church, as the leaders and church members had just appointed a new minister.

At the end of that month, Angie, Ben, Simeon and I had five days away on a canal boat on the Grand Union Canal. The cramped living conditions and the fact that it rained most of the time did not dampen our enthusiasm. Manoeuvring through tunnels and wrestling with locks all added to the fun. We tried to be friendly to the few other canal boats that passed by in the opposite direction. The crew of one boat, though, were so busy concentrating on the conversation they were having with Angie, they crashed at full speed into a bridge. I closed my eyes, asked for forgiveness and turned the throttle up to full power. We sped away.

It became a tradition of ours that whenever one of us had a birthday, we would celebrate by going ten pin bowling and then having a hamburger and a Brown Derby (a delicious mix of doughnut, chocolate sauce and soft ice cream). I was amused and highly embarrassed when on 6th September, the manager presented me with a burger lit with candles. The staff then sang 'Happy Birthday' in front of the other customers. For Angie, revenge was as sweet as the Brown Derby.

With Simeon starting school on a full time basis, I was finding there was not enough to keep me occupied at home and began to look for a job. I considered returning to some form of social work and to enhance my prospects decided to study for a professional counselling qualification. The University of Essex were running a part-time course for mature students and I commenced attending in October. I found studying again both stimulating and challenging. Because of the nature of the course it was necessary to share information about ourselves and our background. One night, after I had shared that I was a house husband a female student said that, 'I was the most sincere feminist she had ever met'. To this day I count that as a compliment.

April 1st was made for practical jokes and Angie and I always tried to creatively rise to the occasion, particularly with our neighbours. In 1995 we decided Garry would appreciate being on the receiving end. We watched Garry leave for work and then placed an old 'For Sale' board in front of his house. We removed the board before he returned home. That evening Garry was perplexed to receive telephone calls from other neighbours to say they were very sorry he was moving house and where was he moving to.

Although the memory of Emily's death was still painful to us, Angie and I felt it was time to move on. We wanted to try and rebuild our lives and felt we were now making real progress. We rarely visited Emily's grave in the cemetery just outside Castle Hedingham and had not therefore had a headstone made. We decided to rectify the situation and contacted a stone mason, Mr Finch, in Braintree to undertake the work. We agreed to keep the headstone simple and small with just her name and dates. Sometimes words cannot adequately express feelings.

Some of the older people who lived in Rosemary Lane had fought in the Second World War. It seemed appropriate that their sacrifices should be remembered and Angie and I decided to organise a VE celebration for all our neighbours. In May about 45 men, women and children gathered on 'Rushley Green'. We shared our food and drink and had sack races. One of the oldest residents made a display board of his medals, which he used as a visual aid to explain to the rest of us about his exploits. We did not want to glorify the war, but to learn about its cost to those who lived a generation ago and be reminded that we should not take the freedoms and opportunities we now enjoy for granted. It was a memorable day.

To celebrate our 20th wedding anniversary, Angie booked a one night break in Stratford on Avon with tickets to see *Romeo and Juliet*. We wanted to remember our visit by having our photo taken. After searching for some time for someone willing to take on the task, an older man finally agreed. It was only after we had given him our camera that we noticed he only had one eye. Fortunately the photograph was in focus and did actually include us.

For our summer holiday, Angie, Ben, Simeon and I decided to have a week on a canal boat on the South Oxford Canal. The canal boat, 'Canberra', was comfortable, but most of the week it rained and we always seemed to moor between a motorway and a railway line. One night when we were looking for somewhere to stop, Ben asked if he could steer the boat. I agreed. It was a mistake. Encouraged by Simeon, Ben deliberately drove the canal boat into the bank and I, taken by surprise, fell overboard and landed bruised and shaken on the tow path. Family life is not always a bed of roses.

But captaining a canal boat was only one of Ben's many skills. He had also discovered that he had a good sense of rhythm and began learning to play the drums.

We thought Simeon might enjoy learning to play the piano, but although he eventually reached Grade 3 he never wanted to practice in between lessons, and his teacher aged considerably over the years he visited.

My search for employment continued. In February 1996 I applied for a part time social work post in Braintree working with older people. Returning to work after a long absence was a daunting experience. I found that the years away from paid employment had undermined my self-confidence. It was a steep learning curve as many of the former work practices/legislation/forms had all changed. Colleagues were supportive but in the end it was only I who could re-engage my brain into work mode. Working part-time also meant I still had responsibility for running the home. Having therefore to cope with two jobs meant the pressures of life rarely eased. The demands on my time were significant. But I made it a priority not to neglect Simeon, Angie or Ben.

One Saturday, Simeon was given a voucher to watch Colchester United play Torquay. Simeon and I soon became totally engrossed in the action. So engrossed that we did not notice when Angie, who was standing behind us, fainted and collapsed to the floor. The stewards were quickly on the scene. As there appeared to be no apparent reason for her fainting, one of the stewards commented, 'It must have been the shock of Colchester scoring a goal!'

In order to fulfil her artistic talents Angie focussed on developing her Batik work. Instead of creating a design, Angie had begun, using the same technique, to produce pictures. In July, Angie exhibited her pictures at the Quay Theatre in Sudbury, a popular arts venue. Many people came to view her work, and although sales were limited, it provided an opportunity for her creativity to be appreciated.

In 1995, Lyn, Simeon's Nursery School leader, had moved with her husband Alan, a banker, to South Africa. Simeon had been keen to visit them, but we had felt the cost of the flights would be more than we could afford. In late July I heard from Oxford University Press that my third children's book had been accepted. The advance on royalties covered the cost of the flights exactly. We arranged to visit the following summer.

Simeon's end of term report in December summed him up in a nutshell. It read, 'Doing well, top Maths Set, good mental tests, sparky, sense of fun'.

Angie and I had always felt that meal times were important in building up relationships and encouraging communication. We made a point therefore of sitting around the table to avoid other distractions. We were aware, though, that meal times could be made more family focussed and so, after lunch on Sundays, we began to play cards with Ben and Simeon in the form of a tournament. After several weeks, the overall winner received a prize. It is a chastening experience as a parent to be constantly beaten in games by your children.

Not only was I learning humility at the hands of my children, I was also learning that at times it is better to say less than more. On offering a female friend a glass of wine, I had, in a joking and over familiar manner said, 'That'll put hairs on your chest'. Her curt reply had been, 'That's already my problem dear'.

In February 1997 Angie, Ben, Simeon and I spent a few days at Centre Parcs in Suffolk. We played snooker and table tennis and went mountain biking. In the swimming complex, Simeon was particularly keen that I go with him on the rapids. Being short-sighted I was afraid of loosing my glasses in the turbulent water. 'Don't worry dad', Simeon said, 'I will look after you.' I took off my glasses and he took me by the hand.

I was well aware that Angie and her colleagues at Beckers Green School worked hard. I knew their evenings, weekends and holidays would often be taken up with lesson preparation, report writing, marking and trying to implement new government initiatives. In early March, the school received its Standard Assessment Tasks (SATS) results. The scores placed the school at the bottom of the league tables in mid Essex. It was clear that focussing mainly on a child's academic ability completely missed the point of education. In a school where the whole child was considered important the results only lowered morale and stifled staff goodwill.

One evening in June, we received a telephone call from Garry to say that a criminal had evaded Police in Castle Hedingham and was last seen heading across the fields toward Rosemary Lane. He advised that we should stay indoors. Some years earlier, Angie and I had purchased a lifelike rubber mask that had the face of an elderly gentleman. We had called the mask 'Mr Wilkins', and used it several times before as a means of tricking people.

We felt this opportunity to hoodwink Garry was too good to miss. Angie donned the mask and a long coat and stood in the field a short distance from Garry's patio doors.

Garry was already in a state of anxiety and when he saw 'Mr Wilkins' immediately phoned the Police to advise them that there was a 'madman' in his garden. Although they had already apprehended the criminal, they agreed to send out the Police helicopter. By the time Garry had finished on the telephone, 'Mr Wilkins' had disappeared. We phoned Garry shortly afterwards to advise him of the ruse. The helicopter was never sent, but Garry had some difficulty explaining to the Police later that he had neighbours who were 'different' from other people.

A few weeks later, however, we were on the receiving end of Garry's unique sense of humour.

Ben required a counter-signature for his passport application. Garry seemed the ideal candidate. He had known Ben for several years, he was a successful business man, honest, caring and hardworking. But we should have known better. As part of his antiques business, Garry immersed secondhand doors in a tank of acid to remove the old paint. When we checked Ben's form, in the box marked 'Profession, professional qualifications or position in the community', Garry had written 'Stripper'.

That summer Angie, Ben, Simeon and I took off from Heathrow on a flight to South Africa. Lyn and Alan were living in a rented house on the outskirts of Johannesburg. As well as a gardener and maid, the house had a swimming pool in the garden and every luxury. It was also surrounded by a large wall and had two automatic iron gates at the front. Inside, at the top of the stairs, was another iron gate that could be locked at night to prevent access to the bedrooms from intruders. It was like living in a prison. In the street every house was the same, except that some had armed guards in sentry boxes in the driveway.

One day, we visited Soweto, a township a few miles away from where we were staying. The streets were mud tracks and the houses were made from corrugated iron. It was like walking through a town of garden sheds. The people were friendly and happy to show us around their homes. The floor was often bare earth perhaps covered with a scrap of carpet to give some sense of 'homeliness'. There was no sanitation, no running water, limited education for the children and few jobs for the adults. They accepted their life of poverty as something they were born into and could not easily change. They were experiencing daily hardships that many in the Western world would not wish on their pets. Their natural charm and good humour could not hide the fact that these people were living without hope. Crime is never justified, but it was easy to see that for some it offered a way of escape. Most wanted a better life, but knew their future lay in decisions made by those whose priorities were not always based on the well-being of others.

We visited the Kruger National Park and the Drakensburg Mountains, where the stars seemed to be within touching distance. We also visited an elderly lady who had prayed for Simeon when he was having his heart surgery. It was an honour to meet someone who did not know us, but whose prayers had had a significant impact on our lives.

For Ben's 18th birthday, Angie and I arranged without Ben knowing for some of his closest friends from the Bude Beach Club team to arrive at the pub where we were having a meal. Being self-assured is important to an older teenager. That night, as people arrived or emerged from hiding in the bar area, Ben's self assurance melted. It was a great reunion.

In November, Simeon's teacher described Simeon as someone who 'doesn't take life seriously'. Simeon wrote about himself, 'I like beef burgers and chips, I like football. My favourite colour is blue. My favourite weather is sun'.

For us, we were just grateful that we had come through another year with him still alive.

CHAPTER SIX

Trina, Ben's babysitter, had followed in her father's footsteps and become an actress. In January 1998 Simeon, Angie and I travelled to a pub in London to see Trina appearing in an adaptation of the 39 Steps. The 'theatre' was a large room above the pub, which meant the venue had plenty of atmosphere. The cast of four were brilliant, although as they each had numerous other parts it was sometimes difficult to work out who was who. The audience, fuelled by alcohol from the bar, were exuberant in their appreciation and often laughed and clapped in the wrong places. But it was live entertainment, and even more entertaining because of its unpredictability.

That visit inspired Simeon to audition for a part in the school's production of Bugsy Malone. Some weeks later, to a packed school hall, Simeon, as the cleaner Fizzy, sang the solo 'Tomorrow Never Comes'. Simeon's stage career had begun.

Ben had decided that rather than go straight to university, he would like to take a gap year. The organisation he had contacted had placed him in a school near Pietersburg in South Africa. In July we took him to Heathrow and he boarded his flight along with several others. We were sad to see him go and Simeon cried all the way home as, despite their age difference, they had grown very close. But we knew it was important for children to have their freedom.

Angie and I, aware that Simeon would miss his brother, that summer booked to stay in one of a group of cottages linked to an activity centre near Tenby, Wales. The site was situated on a cliff top overlooking the sea. The views were magnificent. I have never stayed anywhere that had such an awe-inspiring outlook from the toilet window.

Simeon had his annual check up at the West Suffolk Hospital in the middle of September. He was put through a variety of tests and weighed. The consultant declared that he was making such good progress we would not need to bring him back for three years. Angie and I were delighted. Simeon's yearly hospital MOT had meant we could never really relax. But now the pressure was off.

Although we had good relationships with our neighbours, Angie and I wanted to share our faith with them in a meaningful way. That autumn we arranged to run an Alpha group, a course on basic Christianity, in our home and invited as many people as we could. But nobody came.

During the October half term, Angie, Simeon and I spent a day in London. Apart from visiting Covent Garden we thought St Paul's Cathedral would also be a worthwhile experience. To enjoy the view of London that St Paul's offers we decided to climb right to the top of the dome. Simeon clambered up the many, many, many steps effortlessly. When we finally reached the viewing balcony it was Angie and I who looked and felt as though we were the ones who had had major heart surgery.

On 23rd December a phone call from Ben advised us that he would be arriving at Heathrow earlier than he had anticipated. It was the call we had been waiting for and two hours later we breathlessly arrived in Terminal 2. Our frantic search for Ben, though, proved fruitless mainly because he had been sneaking around behind us all the time. His stay in South Africa had taught Ben a great deal about himself and other people. He had grown up, but not completely. It was only later that we discovered he had been white water rafting along the Zambezi and taken a bungee jump from a bridge near the Victoria Falls.

Simeon had his second major stage performance in the school production of Joseph and his Amazing Technicolor Dreamcoat in March 1999. He was cast as Reuben and Ben played drums to support the music group. For children so young, the performance from all the cast was unforgettable.

One Sunday a speaker named Don Latham came to the Baptist Church. We knew little about him personally, only that he had been a former local authority Chief Executive Officer, First Director of the Society of Local Authority Chief Executives and a non-executive Director in the Heath Service. At the end of the service he invited any one to come to the front of the church so he could pray and lay hands on them. Taking their lead from the minister, many, including Angie, went forward. One by one as Don Latham prayed for the Holy Spirit to come in power upon them, so they fell backwards and lay on the floor. Watching from the balcony, I could see that when he prayed he barely touched people. But the effect was dramatic. Soon the church floor was covered in bodies. After two or three minutes they recovered and went back to their seats. I knew most of the people who had gone forward. The majority were middle-class, middle aged Christians. They did not do extreme Christianity. It was either real, or they had all suddenly become very convincing actors.

Simeon wanted to show Ben where we had had our summer holiday the year before, so in August we travelled back to South Wales. We swam, played golf, did archery and pistol shooting. On a wet day we visited Pembroke Castle and on an even wetter day watched the film, 'The Phantom Menace' in Milford Haven. One of the highlights of the holiday for Angie, Ben and Simeon was a fishing trip in a boat off Tenby. Not because of the number of mackerel we caught, but because the choppy sea made me seasick. I couldn't wait to get back on dry land. Although my father had been in the Royal Navy during the Second World War it was obvious I had not inherited his 'sea legs'.

September brought for Angie and I a beginning and an end. On the 8th Simeon started school at the comprehensive in Sible Hedingham and on the 26th September Ben left for university in Leicester. For the first year Ben was able to have a room in university accommodation and along with many other parents we said our tearful goodbyes, prayed that he would make friends, not stay up all night and also hopefully complete the course. Neither Angie nor I would be disappointed.

By February 2000, Ben had become fully immersed in university life, particularly the Christian Union. He was also considering renting a house for the following two years with three other students Steve, Ben S and Jolly. Angie and I hoped that they would be young men who would not lead Ben astray. We needn't have worried, God had hand picked them. All three were caring, witty and sensitive and they would have the strength of character to support Ben through his darkest moment.

Simeon was also making progress. The school were fortunate enough to have a highly skilled and committed music department. In March, the department put on a concert and the choir, of which Simeon was a member, sang 'America' from the musical West Side Story.

The visit of Don Latham to the Baptist Church had seemed like a turning point, but after some months, Angie and I began to feel a sense of disappointment. The church was continuing to grow numerically, but we felt we could not find there what, deep down, we were thirsting for. A church whose message was not 'comfortable' either for those inside its four walls or for those outside. I discussed the situation with the minister, but found that we had to agree to disagree.

Angie, Ben, Simeon and I began attending the church plant in Great Cornard. Angie and I wondered if God was returning us to where we should have been in 1985 if we had not had the accident. But there was more than that. The worship in the church had a depth we had not experienced in any church. Each Sunday morning a young man named Matt Beales, with a number of other musicians, led the singing and times of prayer. We had never met a worship leader like Matt before. His sensitivity to God enabled the congregation to enjoy a freedom and a joy that lifted you beyond the present. This was not singing songs for the sake of it. Nor routinely repeating what was done the week before. This was enjoying God's presence in a fresh way every time. It was exciting to be in the church services and we were glad to be a part of what God was doing.

During the summer, Angie and I had to make a difficult decision. Roy, the former leader at Sible Hedingham Baptist Church, had divorced his wife and was planning to remarry. Roy knew our feelings on the subject, but being a close friend invited us to the wedding. We could not decide whether to stick to our principles and decline the offer or honour our friendship.

We attended the wedding. Our principles hadn't changed but we decided that being a true friend meant standing by someone whatever the circumstances.

At work, although generally making progress, I found it was becoming increasingly difficult to please all of the people all of the time. Changes in the delivery of public services had meant a rise in client's expectations of what services they should receive. However, often government rhetoric did not match reality and being in the front line, juggling resources sometimes brought you into conflict with those you were trying to help. In June my manager received an unjustified letter of complaint. The 'complaints procedure' was enacted and the matter resolved. But my self-confidence in my ability as a social worker had been seriously undermined. Those making policy decisions are rarely the people who have to cope with the emotional pressure of carrying them out.

I am not the sort of person who has regular 'dreams and visions' about what God is going to do. But that summer, while walking in the garden, a picture came into my mind that was as clear as a picture on a TV screen. I was on a beach and suddenly a tidal wave washed me off my feet. The wave carried all before it, but I did not drown. Indeed, I was enjoying the experience. There was no explanation as to what the picture meant, although I wondered if the tidal wave was the Holy Spirit moving in revival power amongst His church.

Angie and I decided that for our 25th wedding anniversary we wanted to celebrate not only our marriage, but also to thank many of the people who had helped us over the years. We hired a hall in Sudbury and on a beautiful summer's evening welcomed relatives and many friends past and present. Following the meal Angie and I looked back over our experiences. We particularly highlighted the many practical jokes we had played on Garry. His response was to describe us as the 'neighbours from hell!' John Martin performed a humorous monologue and, because we were determined Emily was included in the festivities, a Christian friend who was a professional guitarist played a piece he had written in her memory. Ben closed the evening by praying for us. It was a moving occasion.

And Simeon's contribution to the evening? To remember the event we had asked one of our friends to video the celebration. As people were leaving, Simeon took charge of the video and walked behind them filming their bottoms!

Some years earlier, two of our Christian friends, John and Ann Smith, had moved to live in Collingwood, Ontario about two hours' drive from Toronto. They had offered us the use of their house while they were away. In August Angie, Ben, Simeon and I flew to Toronto, then drove to Collingwood. The house had a substantial garden, several bedrooms and its own snooker room. The back of the house overlooked Georgian Bay, part of Lake Huron. It is the nearest to heaven I have ever been.

We saw chipmunks and a porcupine, learnt about the indigenous Indians and white settlers. Visited an Imax screen and Niagara Falls and Simeon and Ben went to the top of the CN Tower. We were fortunate though to be more than tourists. We met real Canadians and talked about real issues. Canada is a beautiful country and the people friendly. But we were saddened by the fact that because petrol was cheap, most people used their cars for even short journeys. Neither was there a washing line in sight. The majority of people used tumble driers.

Food was also more than plentiful and most kitchens had a huge refrigerator in which to store it. Angie and I were left feeling that those of us in the Western world, because we have more than we need, often do not use what we have wisely and err on the side of waste. Thus any message of restraint we urge on others to reduce the impact of global warming, or advice we give to overcome starvation, is compromised by our own lifestyles. The answer we felt was for those who had too much to reduce their consumption, and enable those with less to gain an acceptable standard of living.

Angie and I were already trying to practice 'simple living' by eating less, not replacing items until we had to, buying things for their usefulness rather than looks and avoiding the lure of 'must have' advertising. Our holiday in Canada made us even more determined to carry on in the same way.

By the end of September Ben, Steve, Ben S and Jolly had found a house to rent in Leicester. The house had a large rear garden, smelly toilet and a small front bedroom which Ben occupied. It was in a street, near the centre of the city, of semi-detached houses, many of which were let to other students. It gave them the freedom to come and go as they please, experience the highs and lows of living in close proximity with others and also an opportunity to develop new skills. Jolly, a politics undergraduate, in order to advance his penchant for horticulture, one day brought home a bay window he had found in a skip with the idea of using it as a greenhouse. As the contraption had limited success he then purchased a propagator to grow mushrooms. However, rather than the mushroom spawn growing into a multitude of individual mushrooms, it grew into one huge mushroom. Unsure what to do with the monstrosity, the four fed it to an unsuspecting visiting speaker to the university Christian Union, who they had invited to tea.

Leicester had a variety of places to dine. On one visit Angie, Ben, Simeon and I could not agree on what type of cuisine we wanted to try. We managed to compromise. Angie and I enjoyed a meal in an Italian restaurant, while Ben and Simeon ate in the Indian restaurant opposite. We were all satisfied.

Scripture Union did not only organise Christian events during the summer holidays in seaside resorts, but also during the rest of the year in cities and urban areas. Because of our past links with the Beach Club in Bude, Angie and I were asked to help with a week long children's club in an area of Leicester known as Belgrave. We felt that it would be a new experience for us and an opportunity to spend some time with Ben.

The area was multicultural, but the church had built up good relationships with those of other faiths and backgrounds. And children are children. They joined in with the songs and activities with real enthusiasm. One day Angie and I visited a Sikh temple. We met the sister of a Sikh leader who had been murdered the week before. She talked about her loss and cried. Inside we cried too. Whatever our colour or creed we are all human beings and at times in our lives we all need support. Religion should never get in the way of compassion.

Ben celebrated his 21st birthday in Leicester. It was a memorable occasion. Not only did the 70 students attending the Christian Union all sing him Happy Birthday and present him with a cake plus candles, when he finally went to bed, Ben found his room filled to the ceiling with balloons!

On 31st December Angie wrote in her diary, 'It's been a good year. I feel we are back on the trodden path and are going somewhere spiritually'. She was right. We knew that if your relationship with God was not on track then no matter what you achieved in this life, you were not investing for eternity. And that was what really mattered. Eternity lasts for a long time.

By February 2001, Simeon was a regular member of a local boy's football team, Hedingham Hawks. Most of their matches were on Sundays, but Angie and I were reluctant for Simeon to miss attending church. The team manager was kind enough to rearrange matches where possible to Sunday afternoons.

For his birthday, Simeon asked if he could have a mixed 'sleep over'. Knowing that the event could produce a whole host of potential disasters, Angie and I planned the evening carefully. First a Bar B Q, then a game of rounders, then Blow out the Candle to tire them out, then to bed in separate accommodation and a peaceful night for everyone. But we miscalculated. Simeon's friends had far more energy than we had anticipated. The girls wanted to spend time with the boys and the boys naturally wanted to spend time with the girls. Angie and I spent the whole night acting as security guards trying to keep them apart. No one slept, but the boys did get some pleasure from sitting in a field and watching the sun rise.

June 10th was Garry's 70th birthday. He did not want a fuss and agreed to go out with his niece for a quiet meal. What Garry did not appreciate was that we had invited all the neighbours to our house for a surprise birthday party. Instead of driving past, their car pulled into our drive. Garry got out of the car and pulled a face. Five years earlier for his 65th birthday, Angie and I had said we would take him to see a play. We collected Garry, but a mile down the road Angie and I had had a row about neither of us having the tickets. Garry politely said nothing. We turned the car round and returned to our house. When we pulled into the drive all the neighbours were waiting in the garden to sing Happy Birthday. Garry had vowed he would never be caught like that again. It was worth the five year wait. All the neighbours who were waiting in the garden, sang Happy Birthday. Déjà vu.

That summer, Angie, Ben, Simeon and I spent a week in a caravan at Stoneleigh, Warwickshire, attending a Bible Week. There were a number of speakers, but only the words of one stuck in our mind. Andy Hawthorne, who worked with young people in Manchester, said, 'There is only one church in the UK. The Church of Jesus'.

As it was some years since we had last been to Scotland, Angie and I felt it would be nice to return and we booked a week's holiday in Fife.

Our accommodation was a converted farm building, which was surrounded by other cottages and a swimming pool and games room. Situated at Kings Barns, near St Andrews, the scenery was spectacular and deserted. Several times the four of us wandered along the empty beach fishing in the rock pools and collecting golf balls. One night we attended the Edinburgh Tattoo. With the castle as a backdrop, the massed pipe bands, Cossack dancers and the audience all singing Auld Lang Syne, the evening was unforgettable. But there were some drawbacks. Ben and Simeon had to sleep together in a double bed. By the end of the week even their 'brotherly love' was being severely tested.

On September 11th Angie and Simeon attended the cardiac clinic in the West Suffolk Hospital. The consultant expressed that Simeon's diagnosis was 'fantastic' and that he would not need to return to the hospital for three years. Our good news, however, was overshadowed by events unfolding around the Twin Towers in New York that were appearing on the television in the hospital waiting room. As Angie and

Simeon celebrated, there were those in the World Trade Centre who were fighting for their lives. Death on such a massive scale is hard to comprehend and the mindset of those who see destroying innocent civilians as something positive, hard to understand. It struck us that, while we were doing everything we could to maintain the life of our son, elsewhere in the world there were others planning to obliterate human lives. One of us obviously had a wrong set of priorities. Unless in self-defence, no-one has the God given right to take the life of another.

Angie and I wanted to encourage Simeon's interest in acting and took him to see a production of Oklahoma. Prior to the performance we met two friends, Dennis and Jenny, in a pizza restaurant. We liked Dennis. Although being a former bank manager he had a sense of humour that rivalled our own. Once, when he was at work, he had left a box on the staff room table. An unsuspecting staff member had lifted the lid and was so surprised by the plastic snake that catapulted itself towards her face, she fainted. Dennis called an ambulance and she was taken to hospital. Fortunately his explanations were sufficient for him to retain his managerial position.

The restaurant was packed with diners. Dennis and Jenny were already seated at a table, and when we arrived stood up to greet us. The fact that Dennis was wearing a long blonde wig so he looked like a woman did surprise us a little, but did not seem to trouble the other patrons who kept on eating, or the staff who took our order without batting an eyelid. Perhaps it happens all the time.

As part of his studies Simeon went on a school trip to the First World War battle fields in Belgium in October. He visited Vimy Ridge, the trenches and the Menan Gate. He learnt about the futility of war, men's obsession with power, and the way, that so often, governments do not learn from their past mistakes. Thus, needless suffering is inflicted again and again and again. It was a sobering experience for us all.

Simeon's appetite for being on stage was becoming insatiable. Towards the end of term, he appeared as the Chief Stoat in a school production of the musical *Toad of Toad Hall* and in December as a 'wise man' in the school's Christmas celebration. Entertaining people and making them laugh was becoming, for Simeon, a way of life.

Following the departure of Andy Jones to a new Headship, Angie began to reconsider her own position and started applying for other teaching posts. In February 2002 she had an interview for a Senior management post at a school in Long Melford, near Sudbury. She was appointed and shortly afterwards left Beckers Green School, taking with her twelve years of her own memories and memories of Simeon.

Angie commenced her new job in April on the same day that Ben and several other Christian students flew to Morocco. They were part of a team seeking to share the Christian faith in that country. Ben found the people welcoming, but the police obstructive and intolerant of 'religious freedom' and 'freedom of speech'.

Angie and I did not want Simeon to take his SATS. We felt it was a time wasting, educationally irrelevant, single-faceted exercise, and advised the school that we would be withdrawing him. It was a difficult decision. We had a good relationship with the staff and felt the school was giving Simeon, as with Ben, a first class education. The teachers were fully aware of Simeon's strengths and weaknesses and did not need a test to confirm them. Simeon's withdrawal did not change the system and in fact adversely affected the school's results. But we felt that colluding with senselessness can never be right.

One Sunday at the church plant in Great Cornard, a man named Brian Gault came to speak. He had written a book called 'Look No Hands' about his life without arms following his mother being prescribed thalidomide during her pregnancy. At the end of the service he signed copies of the book, holding the pen in-between his toes. His message had been, 'God can turn disaster into good'. He was an example that disablement is never an obstacle to living a fulfilled life. It's only the attitudes of the able bodied that often prove to be a barrier. Brian Gault was a living demonstration that removing, by abortion, those who are disabled, deprives the world of many beautiful people.

Whilst on a school holiday, Simeon had put a message in a bottle and thrown it into the sea. The bottle had travelled hundreds of miles and been found by a British soldier in Croatia. The soldier, who lived in Norfolk, had written to Simeon.

The story found its way onto the front page of the Halstead Gazette. He was also interviewed by Essex Radio. Simeon loved being in the limelight.

It was a fitting birthday present for Angie when on July 10th Simeon, Angie and I attended Ben's graduation day at De Montfort Hall in Leicester. It was with great pride that we watched Ben, dressed in mortar board, gown and grey and red silks collect his degree certificate.

That summer, the church plant in Great Cornard held a week long children's holiday club. Each day there was a drama entitled 'Desert Detectives'. Simeon appeared as the character 'Doug' along with the co-star 'Sandy'. Simeon made the part his own. His self confidence was growing as was his talent. The jokes kept coming. Simeon and the audience loved every minute.

Angie and I could not decide whether to have a family holiday. Ben was busy and we were not sure whether a 'threesome' would be successful. At the end of August we travelled to York for a week in a farm cottage. We tried to fill the time in a worthwhile way. We rode on the North York Railway, visited the Jorvik Centre and followed a story teller around the city streets. It was good, but it was not the same. Simeon was now as tall as his brother. He had outgrown his parents not only in height but in preference. He was developing his own tastes.

Angie and I were grateful that whilst living in Rosemary Lane all our neighbours had become close friends. It seemed only right therefore to spend my 50th birthday in the company of those who knew us the best yet still liked us. We spent the evening with Garry and Duncan and his wife Jessica enjoying a meal and remembering the past.

I thought I had kept my birthday a secret from my work colleagues. But social workers are masters at finding out the truth. I arrived at my office to find my desk covered in decorations, balloons adorning my PC and my team mates ready and waiting with a camera to record the event.

Having left university Ben decided to spend a year working for the Universities and Colleges Christian Fellowship as a Relay Worker. This involved helping Christians in universities to organise events and have someone to support them, particularly in their first year. Ben was assigned to the University of East Anglia in Norwich and left to take up his post in September.

Following my experience with the sea off Tenby, Angie felt my fear of being seasick should be confronted. For my birthday Angie had booked four places on the 'Lady Florence', a pleasure boat that took passengers for an early morning trip along the tidal River Alde to view the wild birds and enjoy a three course breakfast. Fortunately the water was dead calm. My breakfast stayed in my stomach.

Throughout the autumn term Simeon rehearsed for his part as Mr Sowerbury, the funeral director in the school production of Oliver. Dressed completely in black, his crowning moment was a rendition of the song, 'It's your funeral'. He and his stage 'wife' sang a duet with great sense of 'tongue in cheek' solemnity. Angie, Ben and I enjoyed the humour of the song, whilst also being aware of its poignancy. It was a mixture of emotions that summed up where we had come from and where after years of struggle we had at last got to.

The final day of the year saw Angie, Ben, Simeon and I enjoying a performance of 'Dick Whittington' at the Mercury Theatre in Colchester. Pantomime at its best proffers acting that is outrageous and humour that is contagious. There was not a dry eye in the auditorium. We laughed and laughed and laughed and laughed. It was a great way to end 2002.

We would not though, as a family, be laughing at the end of 2003.

I had enjoyed the music of 'Madness' since the early 1980s. Somehow Ben and Simeon had become infected by my enthusiasm and early in the new year Angie, Ben, Simeon and I took our seats for a performance of 'Our House', a musical which included many of the group's songs. The music was brilliant, but Angie and I became increasingly uncomfortable with the bad language and blasphemy used by the cast. Disappointed we left for home at the interval. We knew that God was not troubled by innuendo, swearing, or even jokes at His expense. But Angie and I were unhappy that what we had assumed would be 'family' entertainment contained words and actions that we felt were unsuitable for the many children present and added nothing to the story. Our letter to the theatre highlighting the positives and negatives of our visit did not induce a reply.

Angie and I wondered afterwards whether by doing what we did we were being 'intolerant', or that our attitude was 'high handed'. But it seemed to us that a bottom line on behaviour had to be drawn somewhere. Tolerance is fine, but it has its limits. If tolerance means everybody living by their own standards, doing what seems right for them, isn't that anarchy?

Although settled in my work with older people, I began wondering if it was time for a change of employment. I did not feel, though, I could leave my job whilst Oswald was alive. Oswald, a bed bound man in his seventies, suffered from cerebral palsy. He was one of my first clients and over the years I had developed a close relationship with Oswald and his ageing brother, who was his main carer. I had often been asked by other agencies if Oswald should be placed in residential care, for his own well-being. I had resisted their requests, knowing that the relationship between the brothers was so strong and mutually therapeutic, that if broken, it could destroy them both. Consequently, I had initiated a high level of home-care and taken responsibility for the fact that if something went wrong, I would be held accountable. Oswald died at home from natural causes in the spring of 2003. I was now free to change jobs.

Simeon had wanted to extend his opportunities for acting outside of school and had joined the First Call Theatre Group for young people at the Quay Theatre. On 12th March Simeon played Corporal Broughton and a German Soldier in R. C. Sheriff's play about the First World War, *Journey's End*. His school visit to the trenches had given him a real insight into life as a soldier on both sides of the barbed wire fences.

The theatre was full. The four nightly performances from the cast were exceptional. And Simeon wallowed in the praise. He deserved it.

For some months I had been unsettled at the church plant in Great

Cornard. In April I met with the leaders to discuss the situation. The church was continuing to grow numerically, but to grow deeper spiritually I felt there needed to be some new innovations in the church leadership structure. At the end of the meeting, the leaders and I agreed to disagree.

Simeon had been asked to play the part of Pharaoh in a school production featuring songs from Joseph and His Amazing Technicolor Dreamcoat. In preparation, for his presentation, Angie, Ben, Simeon and I travelled to London on 26th April to watch a professional performance of the musical. For the next three months we were to endure Simeon's Elvis impersonations every day.

At the beginning of May, Oxford University Press published my fourth book for children. I was beginning to feel almost famous.

For Simeon's birthday, as part of our birthday tradition, the four of us went ten pin bowling. Simeon was in good form. He scored five strikes in a row and won easily. He enjoyed the candle in his hamburger, but was a little embarrassed when the waiter sang 'Happy Birthday'. At 15 it's not good for your image.

One Sunday in July two of our closest Christian friends, David and Pam, came to lunch. It was a hot day and in the afternoon we decided to sit in the garden and pray together. It was while we were praying a vivid picture came into my mind.

The picture was of a train coming into a station. Having stopped at the buffers, I got off the train and looked around, but the station was filled with darkness. I shared the picture with Pam and David but there seemed to be no explanation to it except that I knew something was going to happen in August.

Having finished his time at the UEA, Ben had decided to take up teaching as a career and applied to join a School Centred Initial Teacher Training (SCITT) course. On 17th July he heard that he had been accepted on the course to commence in September. The 17th July was also a big day for Simeon. That evening he performed 'Song of the King' dressed as Elvis in a specially hired white suit and black wig, to a packed school hall. The audience were ecstatic.

The end of the school year saw Simeon a hero amongst his contemporaries, and amongst the teaching staff a pupil who was making good progress with his GCSEs.

On 19th July Simeon played in the singles finals of the Junior Tennis Tournament in Castle Hedingham. He had already won the tournament for the previous two years and a third win would mean he would equal Ben's achievement nine years earlier. He won the final in style! Their names are both engraved on the Junior Singles Champion trophy.

As we were not having a family holiday Angie and I booked a one night stay in a hotel in Aldeburgh, Suffolk. The hotel was so close to the sea you could lay in bed and listen to the waves. That weekend in August, for the first time since records began, the temperature reached 100°f. Angie and I sat on the beach and swam and relaxed. Having returned home in the evening, I watched a programme about the Brontë sisters. I thought how sad it was that the Rev Brontë had outlived his wife and all their children. It was obvious that even Christians were not immune from trouble.

I wondered if these thoughts were connected to Emily's death. I had decided to stop praying for her to be raised from the dead and on my birthday present list suggested the four of us have a night in a London hotel preceded by a performance of *The Mousetrap*. I was aware that Angie and I had watched the play just a few weeks before Emily had died and having the courage to watch it again seemed a positive way of tying up a loose end.

But that was not the only thing on my mind. My notes on revival had now become a book manuscript. A few publishers had shown an interest, but there was nothing definite. I was frustrated. Very frustrated. In the book I had written about the countless people whose lives were being needlessly destroyed, political ineptitude and corruption even in 'developed' nations and, worst of all, a Christian Church that in many countries was often sidelined and ignored. On 13th August I cried out to God to 'do' something. I pleaded with Him to help. I had done all I could. If He was God, He needed to take the initiative.

On 15th August Simeon was asked to play for the Castle Hedingham Tennis Club C Team. Simeon and his partner Tony were soon five games to one down, but with a supreme effort from both players, managed to win seven games to five! After the match, one of the opponents spoke to Angie and praised Simeon's play on court. Angie explained to him all that Simeon had needed to overcome just to be alive. The man listened to Simeon's story looked Angie in the face and said, 'I can see the pride in your eyes'.

On 16th August we went shopping. Simeon bought a CD by Daniel Bedingfield entitled 'Gotta get thru this'. In the evening Angie, Ben, Simeon and I played snooker and then table tennis. Fooling around, Simeon tipped a whole box of chocolate Celebrations over his head. It was good to be a foursome. To be together. To have fun together.

One of Angie's work colleagues, Fiona, had invited us to her wedding in Belfast on 18th August. We had decided to fly to Northern Ireland the day before and stay overnight in bed and breakfast accommodation. Ben had arranged for Steve, Ben S and Jolly to come and stay while we were away. Simeon was looking forward to having their company and had arranged a special music quiz on the laptop for them to play. There seemed no reason therefore for Angie to be 'heavy hearted' as we left on the morning of the 17th for the airport. I dismissed out of hand Angie's apprehension at leaving Ben and Simeon. I was wrong. I should have listened to Angie. I should have listened to my heart.

Fiona's father met us at the airport. On the way to our accommodation he showed us the graffiti and murals along the Falls Road and the presence of the military. It was a sobering sight. In the evening, before attending the Crescent Church, a Christian fellowship in the heart of Belfast, we had a meal in a fish and chip restaurant. We talked about the future. In conversation Angie said, 'You thought something was going to happen, but nothing has'. I replied, 'August isn't over yet'.

Before going to bed, I phoned Ben to check that all was well. Steve, Ben S, Jolly and another student Martin had arrived and they were all having a great time. Angie and I went to bed knowing that although we had our concerns, our trust was in Almighty God and we could therefore sleep peacefully.

CHAPTER SEVEN

Throughout the night, Angie and I and all the other residents were awakened at regular intervals by someone banging on the front door of our guest house or the telephone ringing. The owner did not live on site and therefore the phone was never answered or the front door opened. We did not suspect anything was wrong, we assumed that it was part of Belfast city night life.

At 7am on Monday 18th August there was a knock on our bedroom door. I innocently turned the key. Two Irish Policemen stood in the doorway. 'Mr and Mrs Jones?' 'Yes'. 'We have some bad news. There has been a death'. 'Who is it?' 'Your son Simeon'.

I stumbled back from the door, almost falling over, feeling faint, nauseous and sweaty. Angie quietly said, 'It's over'. Neither Angie nor I could believe it. We were stunned. But there was no doubt. Our precious son was dead.

The policemen agreed to arrange a flight home and left us. We packed our case in silence. During our trip back to England we barely said a word. We were numb.

Sometime later Ben wrote down the events of what happened after Angie and I had left home.

'Sunday 17th August 2003
My parents left early on Sunday morning to catch their flight to Ireland

leaving Sim and I to get things ready for my four university friends who were coming to stay later that day. As my parents were leaving I noticed that three times my mum said, 'I love you' to my brother and kissed him. We waved them goodbye.

Sim and I were planning to go to church that morning so we quickly made the necessary preparations for 'the boys' and then got in the car and left. We arrived back home from church around lunch time, expecting Ben S, Steve, Jolly and Martin to arrive imminently. They were late but it gave us a chance to get ready. It was a beautiful sunny day so when they arrived we sat outside in the sunshine to eat lunch which I think was a BBQ. About mid afternoon after a lot of chatting and laughing and catching up on news we decided to go for a walk.

The walk took us to Scotch Pastures. We found a large stick at the top of the hill which Sim then threw down the hill. I think we found a golf ball as well that also ended up being chucked down the hill. Some of us ran down the hill to look for it but it was lost. Because I was surrounded by close friends and because Sim was a lot younger than us I thought he was a little isolated. Therefore I walked with Sim and we had the chance to chat one to one. It was good.

After our walk we grabbed a quick meal of cheese and tomato sauce on toast and left for an open air church service in a park in Sudbury. I remember walking into the park with the boys and Sim, dressed in his baggy jeans and baseball cap, thinking he looked good.

Following the service we decided to go to a pub for a drink. We drove to The Swan at Great Henny and after purchasing some drinks went and sat outside on an old pillbox overlooking the river. It was a lovely warm sunny evening. I bought Sim a drink and a packet of McCoys Salt and Malt Vinegar crisps and I remember being glad to have the chance to treat him because I had been working away a lot. After a while Jolly decided he would go inside the pillbox. Sim wanted to go too but I stopped him because I knew he'd get dirty. He was keen to go in, though, so eventually I let him and he had a fun time exploring and messing around.

Around 8pm we left the pub in separate cars. Sim went with Jolly and I took the others. When we arrived back home Jolly and Sim were nowhere to be seen but we had a suspicion that they were hiding somewhere. My mum and dad phoned to check we were all alright. I spoke to them and explained that Sim was hiding somewhere. They never got to speak to him. Eventually Sim and Jolly turned up. They had been sneaking around the house successfully trying to avoid our attention. We hadn't been too bothered as these sorts of antics were the norm. We continued to chat and mess around together.

Later that evening Sim asked me if he could show the boys a PowerPoint quiz that he'd prepared. I thought that they wouldn't be interested so at first I didn't allow him, however I changed my mind and we all sat in the kitchen doing the quiz. Sim really enjoyed showing them and the boys enjoyed doing it.

Throughout the day Sim had been asking me if we could play a certain game with the boys. The game involves two teams and a candle in the middle of the garden. One team goes off in the dark and has to blow out the candle whist the other team has to stop them. It is good fun and Sim loved it. I thought that the boys might feel a little bit old to play the game so although Sim was very enthusiastic I was reluctant to suggest it.

Although it was late (probably about 11pm) and not wanting to disappoint Sim we did suggest playing the game and the boys were keen. We went outside and split into two teams. The first game began and Sim and I were on the same team. Sim was very excited and at one point ran around the garden shouting, 'Melons, melons, melons...' We played a few games swapping over defenders and attackers. After about 40 minutes, we stood in a circle in the middle of the garden to rest and chat about how our team had managed to blow out the candle.

Suddenly, without any warning Sim said, 'I'm going to faint' and he turned and started to run towards the house. After running a few steps he stumbled and collapsed, falling straight to the ground without stopping himself. We went over to him lying there so see if he was alright. I knelt beside him. He did not respond to his name and though I felt for a pulse could not feel one. It was clear that something major was wrong. Sim wasn't breathing and I could hear shallow liquid sounds coming from his mouth.

I quickly told Steve to call an ambulance and he went indoors and did so. He came out of the house a few minutes later and asked me to go and speak to the operator because he didn't know the address, etc. I went to the phone and explained to the operator what was happening outside and they told me what to do in response. I shouted instructions to the boys. Jolly and Martin had had training in administering first aid and they got on and gave Sim mouth to mouth, etc. I asked Ben S to walk to the end of our country lane to wait for the ambulance and he did. We got some blankets to keep Sim warm. Jolly and Martin continued to administer first aid but with little effect. I knew the longer it took the ambulance to get here the less hope there was that Sim would survive.

After about 25 minutes the ambulance did arrived. Two paramedics got out and came into the garden to assess Sim. They cut his clothes with scissors, injected him and I think attached a drip to him that we held. They asked if Sim had had any drink or drugs and we said no. This all took place in the middle of the garden and because there was little light I drove my car into the garden and turned on the headlights to help us see. I remember looking at Sim and feeling sick.

After about 15 minutes and what seemed little response from Sim, the paramedics began to use some portable electric shock equipment to try and get his heart beating. They shocked him on the grass. I don't know if this was successful but they soon moved Sim into the ambulance and we proceeded to the A and E department at Broomfield Hospital, Chelmsford. I travelled in the front of the ambulance and the boys followed behind I think in Jolly's car.

Whilst in the ambulance I talked to the paramedic driver and phoned one of our neighbours. I asked them to break into our house and to get the phone number of the hotel that my parents were staying in. They did do this. I also phoned my auntie and uncle who live in Castle Hedingham. It took me a number of attempts to get through but eventually I did. My uncle apologised for not answering sooner explaining it was because he'd had a few drinks and asked what was wrong with Sim, I said 'a cardiac arrest'. He was shocked and he said he would be at the hospital shortly.

When the ambulance arrived at the hospital we got out and I went into a waiting room with the boys whilst the paramedics took Sim off to an operating room. I was then taken on my own into a small room where a doctor came and explained to me that they were operating on Sim but his chance of survival was small because he had been unconscious for such a long time in the garden. A nurse asked me if I wanted one of the boys to come and sit with me and I asked if she could go and ask Ben S to come and join me.

I prayed with Ben S a little, that God's will would be done and we sat and waited for news. Fairly soon the doctor came back and said that despite their best efforts Sim had died, and even if they had managed to save him it would had been likely that he would have suffered a large amount of brain damage.

All the boys and I were then all taken into another room where we sat and waited. I went to the toilet and when I came back noticed that my auntie and uncle were arriving. They came into the room with the boys and as I hugged my auntie I whispered, 'He didn't make it'. At which she was really shocked because she hadn't realised that the situation was so serious.

We all sat together in the small room and waited. My auntie, despite claiming to be non religious, suggested that we should pray, and we did. Later a nurse came in and asked if we wanted to go and see the body, and although no one was keen I thought that it would be helpful for the boys so I encouraged them to go, and they did. I did this because I remember seeing my sister in the hospital after she had died and it was helpful for me then. After that we said goodbye to the nurses. One gave me their contact details in case I wanted to get in touch. I never did. We all left and went to the cars. I went back with my auntie and uncle and the boys followed in their car. We went to my auntie and uncle's house. We got out camp beds and sleeping bags so we set them up in the lounge and tried to sleep. It was probably around 4am.

I didn't get any sleep and got up about 6.30am. My auntie got up as well and we went outside and she asked me if I thought this would damage my parents' faith. I think I said that I didn't know but I didn't think so. About 7.30am I phoned my parents. I had to try and explain what happened and they seemed quite calm because they were in shock. They told me that they were going to fly back and they'd be home later that afternoon.

My auntie walked her dog up to my house and collected most of the rubbish that had been left by the paramedics, syringe packets, etc. so that it wouldn't be too hard for us when we went back. On her return she then cooked the boys and I a large breakfast.

I left the boys at my aunties and walked back to the house on my own. I moved my car back from the garden and into the drive and I tidied up a small amount of rubbish that was left from the paramedics. I remember picking up an orange rubber cap from the end of a syringe. I tried to make sure that things were pretty much in order before my parents and the boys came back because I wanted to protect them as much as I could from any bad memories. Not long after the boys came back, packed up their things and left around lunchtime.

I was left on my own waiting for my mum and dad to come back. There wasn't really much to do. I laid on my mum and dad's bed so I could look out the window for their car, I played the piano a bit and sang 'Great is the Lord' resolving in my heart to praise God in both good and bad times. I waited. I didn't really feel anything emotionally.

Around 4pm my mum and dad arrived home and I went out to meet them. They were later than they thought because they had got onto the wrong bus at the airport. We stood outside and had a big hug and a cry and then we went into the garden and I explained what happened.

It was hard because I was responsible for Sim and I felt that I had to prove to everyone that his death wasn't my/our fault. To answer people's perceived suspicions that we hadn't actually done anything to cause Sim's death and had indeed done our best to help him. I didn't feel any guilt about it because I know that there wasn't anything we could do, and later learnt that even what we did do was pretty useless given the state that Sim's heart was in.

I think the thing that does hurt and the one thing that I do say to God, especially when I visit Sim's gravestone (that I designed) is, 'Why do you make this life so hard?' And sometimes I cry and God doesn't answer, and in many ways I don't really *need* Him to answer. I just want Him to know that when it comes to my relationship with Sim and what God has put me through in taking him away, its hard. I still trust Him though, totally, 110%, and I know He loves and cares for me 110%, but it's still hard. Life goes on.

I hope that those who read this find it helpful in their life and their walk with God.'

Death can occasion moments of surreality. On August 23rd, the first Saturday after Simeon's death, I drove into our local garage to fill up the car. I looked across the forecourt as I had done many, many times before to the rows of newspapers on display. There, amongst the pictures of the famous and infamous on the front cover of the *East Anglian Daily Times*, was a picture of Simeon smiling, with the accompanying headline, 'TRIBUTES TO SON'S FULL LIFE: Parents remember their beloved boy'. It was reality at its starkest. It was personal grief laid bare for all those walking past. Who, although sympathetic would be, unlike us, carrying on their lives unchanged.

We knew that when he died, Simeon had a faith in God.

On 19th June 2003, he had sent an email to John Prothero's son Tom. Tom was getting married in October and had asked Simeon to be an usher. The email read, 'Hi Tom. Hope you are well. I was in bed late last night and prayed to God to forgive me for something I had done earlier. (But I don't really want to say what it is.) But I wasn't sure whether He had forgiven me or not, so I decided to do a Bible study and the verse I had to look up was 1 John 2; 8-12.

So I looked it up to find out what the verse says, take a look for yourself. It's amazing or you could say an answer to a prayer..... literally!!! I've got a tennis match for the Men's C team in Castle Hedingham tonight, so I shall give God the glory for every game we win or loose because without him I wouldn't be able to play tennis or be alive. I get lots of questions about my religion from my friends, but God helps me to answer as many as I can. I have also been threatened to swear, but I've taken no notice of people who say these things. I know that there is a greater reward in the end, so I don't need to worry about people like them.

There is one question I don't know the answer to:

'Why do bad things happen if God made the world?' Please answer if you can.

Thanks.
Look after yourself.
God Bless.
Sim.'

On 23rd June 2003, Simeon sent another email.

'Hi Tom,
How are your mum and dad getting on? How is the rest of your family?

Thanks for that really encouraging message. Its helped me to feel cool to know that God thinks I'm special. He is really pleased with you too. You have done amazing things, especially going through your school life and still staying a Christian. God must be really proud of you. Don't worry about your life ahead, God has it all planned out, and even when times seem hard, trust in him and he will help you. Read Psalm 27 vs 14 if you ever feel down. I think it will help.

Anyway it's nearly the end of lunch now so I'd better go and get ready for another fun Drama lesson with Mrs Beaumont! YAY!

Take care of yourself.
God Bless,
Sim.'

Simeon's funeral was held at the parish church in Castle Hedingham on 28th August. John Prothero led the service and the 350 strong congregation listened to the many spoken contributions from those who had known Simeon. The worship **group** from the church plant in Great Cornard led the singing and Tom **Prothero** sang a solo. One of our Christian friends, sang a song entitled, 'Child of God'. The words of the chorus have been a comfort to us ever since.

> 'Father You're all I need
> My soul's sufficiency
> My strength when I am weak
> The love that carries me
> Your arms enfold me, till I am only
> A child of God'★

Angie, Ben and I told the congregation our story, but we could not conclude it with a happy ending. Ben prayed with heartfelt grief and when his emotions overtook him, John put a steadying arm around his shoulders. In our hearts, Angie and I wanted Simeon to raise the coffin lid, look out and say, 'Just joking'. We wanted to return to the way things were. A poem written by Angie at the time summed up our collective thoughts and feelings:

> 'The dream broke
> And dashed me onto
> the shore of reality.
> And when I looked at the flotsam and jetsam;
> The wreckage of my life,
> I closed my eyes
> And cried that I might dream again.'

We wanted the nightmare to end. But it was not to be.

The funeral was a fitting tribute to a talented young man and a celebration of his faith. When Simeon was born we had thanked God that He had been gracious enough to give us another child. We had loved him, cared for him and expected him to grow into a reasonably healthy adult. But again there were no answers, only questions. And, despite all Angie, Ben and I had learned from Emily's death, we were faced with the same queries we had been confronted with in 1985. Why us? Twice. We were not angry with God, just puzzled.

★Words and Music by Kathryn Scott (Vineyard Songs (UK/Eire), Vineyard Music Group, Vineyard Ministries International (UK) Ltd, 1999).

Simeon was buried near his sister Emily. The cemetery, surrounded by fields, is a beautifully quiet and peaceful place. From the cemetery gate you can see the comprehensive school in Sible Hedingham where Simeon had enjoyed some of his happiest moments.

In life, Emily and Simeon were three years apart. In death, a few feet. John Prothero said a prayer and threw a few grains of earth onto the coffin. Those who had accompanied us to the graveside stood erect and silent, each one battling with their own thoughts and feelings. For us there was nothing left to say. Angie, Ben and I turned away from the grave, retraced our steps past Emily's headstone and left the cemetery as a threesome.

We had asked people not to send flowers to the funeral, but rather make a donation to a charity called HOPE/HIV, that worked with children in Africa suffering from, or who had been orphaned by, Aids. The donations raised over £1000.

In memory of Simeon, Garry planted a tree on Rushley Green, with a plaque beside it celebrating Simeon's life. Castle Hedingham Tennis Club purchased a wooden bench with the words inscribed on it, 'In love of Sim an ace player'. A plaque was also hung in the foyer of Sible Hedingham Comprehensive School to commemorate Simeon's time there as a pupil.

In total we received 325 cards of condolence and 76 letters. The postman said he had never known such a response. Apart from John Prothero leading the funeral, George Balfour and Roy were also in the congregation. We had at last come full circle. On that special day, our reconciliation with three Christian friends was at last complete.

In September Ben commenced his SCITT course. Angie returned to Long Melford School in October, but the doctor signed me off work indefinitely.

Many of those who attended Simeon's funeral had been in his class. Angie, Ben and I felt that it was important to build on what had been said at the funeral and with the agreement of the leaders at Sible Hedingham Baptist Church, Ben committed himself for three years to running a weekly meeting for young people to talk about the Christian faith. It was well attended and seemed like a good way of achieving something positive from our loss.

But there was something odd about Simeon's death. Why had God warned us beforehand that something was going to happen? Someone pointed out that Simeon had died 40 days before the date of Emily's death. And she had died 40 days before the date of Simeon's discharge from hospital following his heart surgery.

We knew 40 was an important number in the Bible and was always connected with times of testing.

The last date in Simeon's school diary was 18th August. It was almost as if Simeon's death had been deliberately planned.

On the day of the funeral, Mrs Beaumont, Simeon's drama teacher, had given us a piece of paper with the words of Psalm 42 vs 11 written on it, 'But O my soul, don't be discouraged. Don't be upset. Expect God to act! For I know that I shall again have plenty of reason to praise him for all that he will do. He is my help! He is my God'.*

On the day after Simeon's death, Angie and I had both seen the hands on our grandfather clock race around the clock face after the pendulum had fallen off. We had had the clock for 25 years and it had never happened before. It gave both of us the impression of time passing quickly.

God had also spoken to me about a verse in the Bible at the end of the book of Job, concerning how God had given him more daughters, after his other children had all been killed. But what did it all mean? Did it 'mean' anything at all?

Christmas 2003 was a time of painful reality. We celebrated as best we could, but deep down inside the prayer of all three of us was, 'Lord, please take us to be with you as soon as possible so we can be reunited as a family'. We were alive, but we wanted to die. Our minds were full of the question, 'Can a broken life be rebuilt a second time?' If the

*THE HOLY BIBLE, Living Bible Edition, Kingsway Publications Ltd, 1994.

pieces were already chipped, scarred, stained, could God's divine glue ever fashion something that was worthwhile? Lives that again would have some purpose. Some value in the overall scheme of things. We felt, having been there before, that it was a tall order even for God.

Angie, Ben and I kept Christmas presents to a minimum, but friends had given us various gifts. One gift was a book by Dutch Sheets, entitled 'Intercessory Prayer' and subtitled, 'How God Can Use Your Prayers to Move Heaven and Earth' (Regal Books, 1996).

In the opening pages, he told of a woman who, 'was comatose with a tracheostomy in her throat, a feeding tube in her stomach and had been in that condition for a year and a half'. He had prayed for the woman for a whole year. Just when it seemed no progress was being made, the woman 'woke up with full restoration to her brain'.

The point he made was that often Christians are not persistent in prayer. We want answers to our prayers immediately and if we don't get what we ask for, we give up.

For the next year I prayed and fasted. I prayed for Simeon to be raised from the dead and for God to give Angie, Ben and I some direction in our lives. It was hard work, but I was learning the importance of waiting. For a Christian, patience is not a virtue it is a necessity.

In February 2004 Long Melford School had an Ofsted inspection. Angie had experienced the pressure of an inspection before, but this time approached it with a more relaxed attitude. She had a different perspective on life. The lead inspector was particularly positive about Angie's teaching and management skills. His comments built up her self confidence and lit her ambition. Angie had always wanted to be the headteacher of a village school. She began seeking headship vacancies.

Angie was interviewed for the headship at Great Waldingfield School in April. The governors liked her. She liked the governors. It was a marriage made in heaven.

When Simeon died, we had been unsure as to how he could have been given a clean bill of health by the cardiac clinic in 2001 and yet suffered such a catastrophic heart failure. In March we visited Simeon's consultant at the West Suffolk Hospital. He explained that Simeon did not die from problems relating to his heart surgery, but from ventricular fibrillation, an electrical problem in his heart which had caused it to stop beating. Death would have been virtually instantaneous. It was almost as if someone had flicked the switch of his heart to off. And maybe someone had.

We decided to purchase a headstone for Simeon and asked Ben who was teaching in Sudbury to visit a stonemasons on our behalf. There were several in the town, but Ben went to the one nearest to the school. His name sounded familiar. It should have done. It was Mr Finch who had moved from Braintree some years earlier. With his help Ben designed the headstone. The text on it reads, 'Your real life is in heaven with Christ and God'.★

West Mersea Free Church, where Andy Jones was a leader, had started an alternative evening service called 'Causeway'. Mainly for older teens or twenty something's but really open to anyone who was prepared to accept 'church' done in a different way. The music was meaningful, the setting relaxed but respectful and the service presented the Christian message in a variety of ways. From drama to comedy, from personal testimony to small group discussion. From quiet individual prayer to Bible teaching. It was innovative, alive, challenging and successful. It was church as it should be. Angie, Ben and I were asked to talk about suffering. We shared our experiences and answered questions. It was painful but at the same time a release. We hoped what we said would help others.

It did. But what we saw and heard helped us far more. We were particularly encouraged by two young men, Joe and Tom. Adopted twin brothers who had been destroying their lives with a mixture of alcohol, drugs and sex. But they had become Christians and their lifestyle had been totally transformed.

Ben successfully completed his SCITT course in July and in August

★Colossians 3:3, THE HOLY BIBLE, Living Bible Edition, Kingsway Publications Ltd, 1994.

took some of his young people's group to 'Soul in the City', a Christian event in London that attracted thousands of teenagers. The aim was to teach them about the Christian faith and then provide opportunities in London for the teenagers to share that faith in practical ways.

Following Simeon's death I had felt the need for a change of direction and decided during the year not to return to social work. I had no other job to take up and was unsure of which path to follow, except that of maintaining the house in a manner to which Angie had become accustomed; and to wait.

Being at home proved to be advantageous when in September Angie took up her new post. Leading a school proved to be demanding. Although only teaching part of the week, she also had to manage the budget, the staff, promote good communication between the school and the parents and ensure educational standards were maintained. It was a steep learning curve, but Angie rose to the occasion and with each week grew in confidence.

For one of my birthday presents Angie, Ben and I had a one night stay in Bawdsey Manor, a large Victorian house on the Suffolk coast near Woodbridge. It had beautiful views of the sea and its own snooker room, but being a threesome evoked too many memories. Walking along the solitary beaches gave us too much time to think about the past. We just prayed that somehow God would move us forward.

By November, Angie and I had decided that it was time to leave the church plant in Great Cornard. Unfortunately our differences with those in leadership could not be resolved. We did not have another church to go to and concluded that, for the time being, we would have to walk with Jesus on our own. We just seemed unable to compromise when we felt wrong decisions were being made.

Ben's youth group was growing and the church leaders decided that although within the congregation there was no one of a suitable age to help, they would be willing to pay for a youth worker to support him. An organisation in Braintree, Christian Youth Outreach, had a young woman available named Sarah. She was experienced in working with young people and had had contact with schools in the area. She seemed like an ideal choice. She was. Not only would she be able to help Ben manage his work with the young people, she would be God's provision for a lifelong partner.

Angie had been searching for somewhere she and I could have time away when we felt like a break. In May 2005 we arrived at Deer Park Cottage, in North Norfolk. It was a converted farm building situated on a large country estate. The farmer raised deer to sell as venison and had large herds roaming the parkland. It was love at first sight. Being near to the coast, it offered walking, peace and quiet and homely accommodation to return to.

Angie and I visited the cottage again in October. For Angie it offered a chance to relax, for me, a chance to think and pray. Since Simeon's death I had continued writing about revival. A publisher had told me that my manuscript was really three books in one. I decided to separate the books and make them complete in their own right. I noticed a theme running through all three. It was this. The Holy Spirit is coming in a new outpouring, to prepare the way for the return of King Jesus. But God never puts new wine into old wine skins.

On February 14th 2006, Valentine's Day, Ben proposed to Sarah in the field overlooking his primary school in Castle Hedingham. They have asked John Prothero to officiate at their wedding service. Sarah is a beautiful girl. Both inwardly and outwardly. She is smart, has a cheeky grin and large brown eyes. She has become like a daughter to us.

Together, on March 12th Ben and Sarah led a Sunday evening youth event at Sible Hedingham Baptist Church. It included a variety of items and Ben spoke at the end. He concluded with the words, 'I hope that people will say in years to come, we have been doing a good work'.

Their 'good work' and perseverance has not been in vain. Simeon's death has been a catalyst for 'new life' amongst a number of his peers.

Deserts are unfriendly places. You have to keep walking or you die. You are unsure where you have been and often have little idea where you are going. The terrain is hard and uncharted. There is no road map. Every step is a step onto virgin soil. And if the uncertainty of the future isn't enough to cope with, although you try your best, you also get blisters on your feet.

Much of our married life has been a desert experience. Untimely death propels you into a desert, with no survival training and no easy to read manual to help you manage. Others can initially support you on the journey, but they can only come so far. In time you have to walk alone and personally endure the loneliness that separation brings. And the blisters of life, the bills, the aches and pains, unhelpful criticism, damp dreary mornings, become your only companions.

But deserts are not all bad. They can be places to find yourself. To find God. And when you reach the other side of the desert, you are softer on the inside, tougher on the outside and see the world from a different perspective. Deserts are places of solitude, but can also be places of hope. Places of learning. They may be places of difficulty, but they do not have to be places of defeat.

What then have Angie and I learnt from our experiences?

To think more deeply. To hate robbery in all its forms, whether it is the theft of personal belongings, unnecessary loss of life or liberty, or a nation exploiting the natural resources and talent of another country. To trust that although we do not always understand what's happening, God never abandons us. To appreciate that life cannot be neatly packaged. We can plan, but we can have no guarantee that what we are aiming for in this life will come to pass.

That the question, 'why us' can only be answered by another question. Why not us? Sometimes we just have to let God be God and believe that He knows what He is doing. Thus, there is never any value in looking back with regret. We need to look forward with hope. To take every opportunity to say 'I love you', to those we are close to.

All these thoughts and feelings have now taken their place in our psyche. But more, much more, we have learnt that the pressing need in these days, in a suffering fragmented world, where daily many endure loss and heartache, is not only to lamely ask the question 'why are things the way they are?' but to seek, wherever possible, to improve the situation, at whatever the cost.

Many people in this life, be it through disability, poverty, accident or illness, have their own hardships to bear. For Angie and I it has concerned two of our children and brought us intense pain and, at times, unbearable missing. For us, though, Emily's death has been more than just another road traffic statistic, Simeon just another name on a hospital waiting list. For our eyes have been opened to a world that previously only existed at a distance.

Our frequent trips to Guy's Hospital to visit Simeon, often took us along the Mile End Road. We could not help but notice the seeming deprivation at one end and the display of amassed wealth at the other. It highlighted for us the total injustice in the world. Man made injustice that traps people not only in physical poverty, but spiritual poverty. Injustice that must be challenged and changed.

But that will not happen the way things currently are in the Christian Church or society in general.

So what is God's message? It is a message that confirms He is there. It is a message that He can bring good out of bad. It is a message about the importance of relationship. Our relationship with Him. Our relationships with each other. It is a message about self-imposed pride that hinders unity. It is a message that love for God and obedience to His commands go hand in hand. It is a message of a revived, transformed church and a better society. It is a message of living with and embracing change.

But even though change is a fact of life, to change can be a painful process, and therefore we often only accept it grudgingly. We accept change in our minds and acknowledge it, but at the same time resent its intrusion.

God wants His Church to change. God wants society to change. But that can only happen if people are committed to change with the whole of their being. A motivation to put right what's wrong that comes from deep down inside them.

So God's message is this. The world is ripe for change. But little will be achieved if the inspiration to move forward comes solely from our minds alone.

It is time for a revolution. It is time for a change

It is time for a change of HEART.

But how does God's message work out in practical terms?
What specifics need to be addressed?
What issues resolved?
What in real terms needs to change?

The message continues in two further titles:

Turning the Tide – God's Heart Surgery for His Church
and
Turning the Tide – God's Heart for the Nation

Printed in the United Kingdom by
Lightning Source UK Ltd., Milton Keynes
139152UK00001B/54/A